D1489917

ON TRANSLATING HOMER

BY

MATTHEW ARNOLD

Prophets of Sensibility:

Precursors of Modern Cultural Thought

GENERAL EDITOR

PROFESSOR HAROLD BLOOM
YALE UNIVERSITY

CHELSEA HOUSE
NEW YORK 1983

PROPHETS OF SENSIBILITY: PRECURSORS OF MODERN CULTURAL THOUGHT

by Harold Bloom
Professor of the Humanities
Yale University

It was one of the peculiarities of literary Modernism, in the Age of Pound, Joyce and Eliot, and of their New Critical followers, to argue that the imaginative literature of the twentieth century had its true origins in seventeenth-century sensibility. In this polemical contention, Eliot could insist that his poetic and critical stance, or more simply his personal culture, had its sources in Lancelot Andrewes and John Donne, rather, say, than in Walter Pater and Matthew Arnold. Assertions of a remote ancestry have the special charm of escaping the immediate squalors of the family romance. We need not smile too ironically at the personal mythologies of an Eliot or a Pound when we reflect upon the even more formidable Sigmund Freud, who in *Beyond the Pleasure Principle* cheerfully proclaims his descent from Empedocles, safely distant at two millennia, while stubbornly denying his palpable precursor, Arthur Schopenhauer.

But the wry humor of these necessary stratagems of the spirit cannot be allowed to obscure the truth of intellectual and aesthetic genealogy. Wallace Stevens once remarked that genealogy is the art of correcting other genealogists' mistakes. One broad way of characterizing the Prophets of Sensibility series is to observe that it intends to correct Eliot's persuasive misreading of the family relationship between nineteenth- and twentieth-century thought and literature. A book like Walter Pater's early masterpiece, *The Renaissance,* reverberates endlessly in such characteristic modern creators as Yeats, Eliot, Joyce, Pound, Stevens, Woolf, Hart Crane, and even in a vitalistic heretic like D. H. Lawrence. None of them (except for Yeats) would have granted Pater's authority and fatherhood, yet he haunts them all (and many others) both in cadence and in concept. Pater, like Arnold, Ruskin, Carlyle, Butler, Hazlitt, De Quincey, and Coleridge is simply too close for the comfort of autonomy to assert itself.

Certainly the anxiety of influence is a crucial sorrow in the vexed story of the true heritage of Modernism. But, as an anxiety, it may conceal deeper continuities between Romantic and Victorian forerunners and their belated heirs. Prophecy, an ancient Hebraic mode of literature, became in the nineteenth century a new kind of vitalistic mode, one that erased the always wavering boundaries between criticism and creation. What, after all, is the literary genre of Pater's *The Renaissance?* The prose *Imaginary Conversations* of Landor and the verse monologues of Browning are no more radical as experiments than are these reveries of Walter Pater. Pater blends moral reflection, prose poetry, psychological portraiture, art and literary criticism, cultural history and a curious kind of mythopoeic fiction into an amalgam that defies conventional description, but that has the ultimate purpose of subverting Christian evaluations of the *agon* between the desires of this world and the work of the spirit. As a prophet, Pater restores to art the epiphanies appropriated by orthodox dualisms, whether of religion or of philosophy.

Pater's *The Renaissance* dramatizes the authentic burden of the Prophets of Sensibility. This burden is not so much secularization as it is the problematic transferences and descents of authority from earlier times, when it could be recognized and accepted, to the threshold of our age, where authority can be recognized precisely as what has vanished, and what could not be accepted if somehow it reappeared. Freud, who devised the clinical transference of the model of the taboo, attempted to make of psychoanalysis a modernist *praxis* that would reestablish the images of authority upon a supposedly scientific basis. Ruskin, Carlyle, Pater and the other Victorian prophets assumed, rather, that authority could be established again only upon an aesthetic basis. Had Freud (and Nietzsche) written in English, we would group them now with the Prophets of Sensibility. Science and philosophy, like religion, have yielded to the literary culture, and the pragmatic consequences of that yielding are at the center of Romantic and Victorian prophecy.

Prophecy, in the Hebraic sense, was moral truth-telling of the most violent kind, always following the formula of "The Word of God came to me . . ." The God Word that came to the nineteenth-century prophets mixed perception and sensation into a new kind of sensibility, one that is still with us today. Difficult to describe, this sensibility emphasizes a continuum haunted by intimations of mortality punctuated by brief bursts of radiance–privileged moments in which a peculiar vividness gives the illusion of redeeming life. It may be the stigma of the nineteenth-century Prophets of Sensibility that (except for Pater) they sought to combat this climate of the spirit but oddly fostered it implicitly (even as Pater did so overtly). The increasing internalization of the self depended upon an augmentation of estrangement from the object world, and what was intended as prophetic warning and lament as to this estrangement became instead a subtle suggestion of an inevitable movement in elite sensibility.

Today we have the strange anomaly that Nietzsche, the Continental version of the Prophets of Sensibility, is credited with fathering the future, while the

Prophets are neglected. But time's revenges work themselves out, and these writers will father the future again, even as they prophesied our current sensibility. They could not save or even preserve the post-Christian spirituality they sought to imbue in society, but they fostered in its place a pragmatic triumph of literary culture, beyond religion and beyond speculative philosophy. Psychoanalysis, despite its scientism, is only another form of that literary culture. So, in another way, are the textualist literary criticism and language-oriented "human sciences" that are vivid parts of Structuralist and post-Structuralist formulations. There are true and false prophets of sensibility, even as there were true and false prophets among the ancient Hebrews. The test for prophecy finally is canonization; the books that return from the dead certify themselves as inescapable, and so as a vital part of the truth. We can say of each of us in relation to the books in this Prophets of Sensibility series what Pater said of his hero in *Marius the Epicurean*. The experience of reading them

> . . . gave him a definitely ascertained measure of his moral or intellectual need, of the demand his soul must make upon the powers, whatsoever they might be, which had brought him, as he was, into the world at all. . . .

ON TRANSLATING HOMER.

. . . . Nunquamne reponam?

I.

It has more than once been suggested to me that I should translate Homer. That is a task for which I have neither the time nor the courage; but tho suggestion led me to regard yet more closely a poet whom I had already long studied, and for one or two years the works of Homer were seldom out of my hands. The study of classical literature is probably on the decline; but, whatever may be the fate of this study in general, it is certain that, as instruction spreads and the number of readers increases, attention will be more and more directed to the poetry of Homer, not indeed as part of a classical course, but as the most important poetical monument existing. Even within the last ten years two fresh translations of the *Iliad* have appeared in England: one by a man of great ability and genuine learning, Professor Newman; the other by Mr. Wright, the conscientious and painstaking translator

of Dante. It may safely be asserted that neither
of these works will take rank as the standard translation of Homer; that the task of rendering him
will still be attempted by other translators. It
may perhaps be possible to render to these some
service, to save them some loss of labour, by pointing
out rocks on which their predecessors have split,
and the right objects on which a translator of Homer
should fix his attention.

It is disputed what aim a translator should propose
to himself in dealing with his original. Even this
preliminary is not yet settled. On one side it is
said that the translation ought to be such "that
the reader should, if possible, forget that it is a
translation at all, and be lulled into the illusion
that he is reading an original work,—something
original" (if the translation be in English), "from
an English hand." The real original is in this case,
it is said, "taken as a basis on which to rear a poem
that shall affect our countrymen as the original may
be conceived to have affected its natural hearers."
On the other hand, Mr. Newman, who states the
foregoing doctrine only to condemn it, declares
that he "aims at precisely the opposite: to retain
every peculiarity of the original, so far as he is able,
*with the greater care the more foreign it may happen to
be;*" so that it may "never be forgotten that he is
imitating, and imitating in a different material." The
translator's "first duty," says Mr. Newman, "is a
historical one, to be *faithful*." Probably both sides
would agree that the translator's "first duty is to

be faithful;" but the question at issue between them is, in what faithfulness consists.

My one object is to give practical advice to a translator; and I shall not the least concern myself with theories of translation as such. But I advise the translator not to try "to rear on the basis of the *Iliad*, a poem that shall affect our countrymen as the original may be conceived to have affected its natural hearers;" and for this simple reason, that we cannot possibly tell *how* the *Iliad* "affected its natural hearers." It is probably meant merely that he should try to affect Englishmen powerfully, as Homer affected Greeks powerfully; but this direction is not enough, and can give no real guidance. For all great poets affect their hearers powerfully, but the effect of one poet is one thing, that of another poet another thing: it is our translator's business to reproduce the effect of Homer, and the most powerful emotion of the unlearned English reader can never assure him whether he has *re*produced this, or whether he has produced something else. So, again, he may follow Mr. Newman's directions, he may try to be "faithful," he may "retain every peculiarity of his original;" but who is to assure him, who is to assure Mr. Newman himself, that, when he has done this, he has done that for which Mr. Newman enjoins this to be done, "adhered closely to Homer's manner and habit of thought"? Evidently the translator needs some more practical directions than these. No one can tell him how Homer affected the Greeks; but there are those who can tell him how Homer

affects *them*. These are scholars; who possess, at
the same time with knowledge of Greek, adequate
poetical taste and feeling. No translation will seem
to them of much worth compared with the original;
but they alone can say whether the translation produces more or less the same effect upon them as the
original. They are the only competent tribunal in
this matter: the Greeks are dead; the unlearned
Englishman has not the data for judging; and no
man can safely confide in his own single judgment
of his own work. Let not the translator, then,
trust to his notions of what the ancient Greeks
would have thought of him; he will lose himself
in the vague. Let him not trust to what the ordinary English reader thinks of him; he will be taking
the blind for his guide. Let him not trust to his
own judgment of his own work; he may be misled
by individual caprices. Let him ask how his work
affects those who both know Greek and can appre-
ciate poetry; whether to read it gives the Provost
of Eton, or Professor Thompson at Cambridge, or
Professor Jowett here in Oxford, at all the same
feeling which to read the original gives them. I
consider that when Bentley said of Pope's translation, "It was a pretty poem, but must not be called
Homer," the work, in spite of all its power and
attractiveness, was judged.

Ὡς ἂν ὁ φρόνιμος ὁρίσειεν,—"as the judicious
would determine,"—that is a test to which every
one professes himself willing to submit his works.
Unhappily, in most cases, no two persons agree as

to who "the judicious" are. In the present case, the ambiguity is removed : I suppose the translator at one with me as to the tribunal to which alone he should look for judgment; and he has thus obtained a practical test by which to estimate the real success of his work. How is he to proceed, in order that his work, tried by this test, may be found most successful ?

First of all, there are certain negative counsels which I will give him. Homer has occupied men's minds so much, such a literature has arisen about him, that every one who approaches him should resolve strictly to limit himself to that which may directly serve the object for which he approaches him. I advise the translator to have nothing to do with the questions, whether Homer ever existed ; whether the poet of the *Iliad* be one or many ; whether the *Iliad* be one poem or an *Achilleis* and an *Iliad* stuck together ; whether the Christian doctrine of the Atonement is shadowed forth in the Homeric mythology ; whether the Goddess Latona in any way prefigures the Virgin Mary, and so on. These are questions which have been discussed with learning, with ingenuity, nay, with genius ; but they have two inconveniences,—one general for all who approach them, one particular for the translator. The general inconvenience is that there really exist no data for determining them. The particular inconvenience is that their solution by the translator, even were it possible, could be of no benefit to his translation.

I advise him, again, not to trouble himself with constructing a special vocabulary for his use in translation; with excluding a certain class of English words, and with confining himself to another class, in obedience to any theory about the peculiar qualities of Homer's style. Mr. Newman says that "the entire dialect of Homer being essentially archaic, that of a translator ought to be as much Saxo-Norman as possible, and owe as little as possible to the elements thrown into our language by classical learning." Mr. Newman is unfortunate in the observance of his own theory; for I continually find in his translation words of Latin origin, which seem to me quite alien to the simplicity of Homer, — "responsive," for instance, which is a favourite word of Mr. Newman, to represent the Homeric ἀμειβόμενος :

"Great Hector of the motley helm thus spake to her *responsive*.
"But thus *responsively* to him spake god-like Alexander."

And the word "celestial," again, in the grand address of Zeus to the horses of Achilles,

"You, who are born *celestial*, from Eld and Death exempted !"

seems to me in that place exactly to jar upon the feeling as too bookish. But, apart from the question of Mr. Newman's fidelity to his own theory, such a theory seems to me both dangerous for a translator and false in itself. Dangerous for a translator; because, wherever one finds such a theory announced (and one finds it pretty often), it is generally followed by an explosion of pedantry; and pedantry is of all things in the world the most un-Homeric. False in

itself; because, in fact, we owe to the Latin element
in our language most of that very rapidity and clear
decisiveness by which it is contradistinguished from
the German, and in sympathy with the languages of
Greece and Rome : so that to limit an English translator of Homer to words of Saxon origin is to deprive
him of one of his special advantages for translating
Homer. In Voss's well-known translation of Homer,
it is precisely the qualities of his German language
itself, something heavy and trailing both in the struc-
ture of its sentences and in the words of which it is
composed, which prevent his translation, in spite of
the hexameters, in spite of the fidelity, from creating
in us the impression created by the Greek. Mr.
Newman's prescription, if followed, would just strip
the English translator of the advantage which he has
over Voss.

The frame of mind in which we approach an author
influences our correctness of appreciation of him ; and
Homer should be approached by a translator in the
simplest frame of mind possible. Modern sentiment
tries to make the ancient not less than the modern
world its own ; but against modern sentiment in its
applications to Homer the translator, if he would feel
Homer truly—and unless he feels him truly, how can
he render him truly?—cannot be too much on his
guard. For example : the writer of an interesting
article on English translations of Homer, in the last
number of the *National Review*, quotes, I see, with
admiration, a criticism of Mr. Ruskin on the use of
the epithet φυσίζοος, " life-giving," in that beautiful

passage in the third book of the *Iliad*, which follows
Helen's mention of her brothers Castor and Pollux
as alive, though they were in truth dead :

> ὣς φάτο · τοὺς δ' ἤδη κατέχεν φυσίζοος αἶα
> ἐν Λακεδαίμονι αὖθι, φίλῃ ἐν πατρίδι γαίῃ.[1]

"The poet," says Mr. Ruskin, "has to speak of the
earth in sadness ; but he will not let that sadness
affect or change his thought of it. No ; though
Castor and Pollux be dead, yet the earth is our
mother still,—fruitful, life-giving." This is a just
specimen of that sort of application of modern sentiment to the ancients, against which a student, who
wishes to feel the ancients truly, cannot too resolutely
defend himself. It reminds one, as, alas ! so much
of Mr. Ruskin's writing reminds one, of those words
of the most delicate of living critics : " Comme tout
genre de.composition a son écueil particulier, *celui du
genre romanesque, c'est le faux.*" The reader may feel
moved as he reads it ; but it is not the less an example of " le faux " in criticism ; it is false. It is not
true, as to that particular passage, that Homer called
the earth φυσίζοος, because, " though he had to speak
of the earth in sadness, he would not let that sadness
change or affect his thought of it," but consoled himself by considering that " the earth is our mother
still,—fruitful, life-giving." It is not true, as a
matter of general criticism, that this kind of senti-
mentality, eminently modern, inspires Homer at all.
"From Homer and Polygnotus I every day learn

[1] *Iliad*, iii. 243.

more clearly," says Goethe, "that in our life here above ground we have, properly speaking, to enact Hell:"[1]—if the student must absolutely have a key-note to the *Iliad*, let him take this of Goethe, and see what he can do with it; it will not, at any rate, like the tender pantheism of Mr. Ruskin, falsify for him the whole strain of Homer.

These are negative counsels; I come to the positive. When I say, the translator of Homer should above all be penetrated by a sense of four qualities of his author;—that he is eminently rapid; that he is eminently plain and direct, both in the evolution of his thought and in the expression of it, that is, both in his syntax and in his words; that he is eminently plain and direct in the substance of his thought, that is, in his matter and ideas; and, finally that he is eminently noble;—I probably seem to be saying what is too general to be of much service to anybody. Yet it is strictly true that, for want of duly penetrating themselves with the first-named quality of Homer, his rapidity, Cowper and Mr. Wright have failed in rendering him; that, for want of duly appreciating the second-named quality, his plainness and directness of style and dictation, Pope and Mr. Sotheby have failed in rendering him; that for want of appreciating the third, his plainness and directness of ideas, Chapman has failed in rendering him; while for want of appreciating the fourth, his nobleness, Mr. Newman, who has clearly seen some of the faults of his predecessors, has yet failed more conspicuously than any of them.

[1] *Briefwechsel zwischen Schiller und Goethe*, vi. 230.

Coleridge says, in his strange language, speaking of the union of the human soul with the divine essence, that this takes place

" Whene'er the mist, which stands 'twixt God and thee,
    Defecates to a pure transparency ; "

and so, too, it may be said of that union of the translator with his original, which alone can produce a good translation, that it takes place when the mist which stands between them—the mist of alien modes of thinking, speaking, and feeling on the translator's part—"defecates to a pure transparency," and disappears. But between Cowper and Homer—(Mr. Wright repeats in the main Cowper's manner, as Mr. Sotheby repeats Pope's manner, and neither Mr. Wright's translation nor Mr. Sotheby's has, I must be forgiven for saying, any proper reason for existing) —between Cowper and Homer there is interposed the mist of Cowper's elaborate Miltonic manner, entirely alien to the flowing rapidity of Homer ; between Pope and Homer there is interposed the mist of Pope's literary artificial manner, entirely alien to the plain naturalness of Homer's manner ; between Chapman and Homer there is interposed the mist of the fancifulness of the Elizabethan age, entirely alien to the plain directness of Homer's thought and feeling ; while between Mr. Newman and Homer is interposed a cloud of more than Egyptian thickness,—namely, a manner, in Mr. Newman's version, eminently ignoble, while Homer's manner is eminently noble.

I do not despair of making all these propositions

clear to a student who approaches Homer with a free mind. First, Homer is eminently rapid, and to this rapidity the elaborate movement of Miltonic blank verse is alien. The reputation of Cowper, that most interesting man and excellent poet, does not depend on his translation of Homer ; and in his preface to the second edition, he himself tells us that he felt,— he had too much poetical taste not to feel,—on returning to his own version after six or seven years, "more dissatisfied with it himself than the most difficult to be pleased of all his judges." And he was dissatisfied with it for 'the right reason,—that "it seemed to him deficient *in the grace of ease."* Yet he seems to have originally misconceived the manner of Homer so much, that it is no wonder he rendered him amiss. "The similitude of Milton's manner to that of Homer is such," he says, "that no person familiar with both can read either without being reminded of the other ; and it is in those breaks and pauses to which the numbers of the English poet are so much indebted, both for their dignity and variety, that he chiefly copies the Grecian." It would be more true to say : "The unlikeness of Milton's manner to that of Homer is such, that no person familiar with both can read either without being struck with his difference from the other ; and it is in his breaks and pauses that the English poet is most unlike the Grecian."

The inversion and pregnant conciseness of Milton or Dante are, doubtless, most impressive qualities of style ; but they are the very opposites of the direct-

ness and flowingness of Homer, which he keeps alike
in passages of the simplest narrative, and in those of
the deepest emotion.   Not only, for example, are
these lines of Cowper un-Homeric :—

> " So numerous seemed those fires the banks between
>   Of Xanthus, blazing, and the fleet of Greece
>   In prospect all of Troy ; "

where the position of the word "blazing" gives an
entirely un-Homeric movement to this simple passage,
describing the fires of the Trojan camp outside of
Troy; but the following lines, in that very highly-
wrought passage where the horse of Achilles answers
his master's reproaches for having left Patroclus on
the field of battle, are equally un-Homeric :—

> " For not through sloth or tardiness on us
>   Aught chargeable, have Ilium's sons thine arms
>   Stript from Patroclus' shoulders ; but a God
>   Matchless in battle, offspring of bright-haired
>   Latona, him contending in the van
>   Slew, for the glory of the chief of Troy."

Here even the first inversion, "have Ilium's sons
thine arms Stript from Patroclus' shoulders," gives
the reader a sense of a movement not Homeric ; and
the second inversion, "a God him contending in the
van Slew," gives this sense ten times stronger.   Instead of moving on without check, as in reading the
original, the reader twice finds himself, in reading the
translation, brought up and checked.   Homer moves
with the same simplicity and rapidity in the highly-
wrought as in the simple passage.

It is in vain that Cowper insists on his fidelity :

"my chief boast is that I have adhered closely to my original:"—"the matter found in me, whether the reader like it or not, is found also in Homer; and the matter not found in me, how much soever the reader may admire it, is found only in Mr. Pope." To suppose that it is *fidelity* to an original to give its matter, unless you at the same time give its manner; or, rather, to suppose that you can really give its matter at all, unless you can give its manner, is just the mistake of our pre-Raphaelite school of painters, who do not understand that the peculiar effect of nature resides in the whole and not in the parts. So the peculiar effect of a poet resides in his manner and movement, not in his words taken separately. It is well known how conscientiously literal is Cowper in his translation of Homer. It is well known how extravagantly free is Pope.

> "So let it be !
> Portents and prodigies are lost on me:"

that is Pope's rendering of the words,

> Ξάνθε, τί μοι θάνατον μαντεύεαι; οὐδέ τί σε χρή·[1]
> "Xanthus, why prophesiest thou my death to me? thou needest not at all:"—

yet, on the whole, Pope's translation of the *Iliad* is more Homeric than Cowper's, for it is more rapid.

Pope's movement, however, though rapid, is not of the same kind as Homer's; and here I come to the real objection to rhyme in a translation of Homer. It is commonly said that rhyme is to be abandoned in a translation of Homer, because "the exigences of

[1] *Iliad*, xix. 420.

rhyme," to quote Mr. Newman, "positively forbid
faithfulness;" because "a just translation of any
ancient poet in rhyme," to quote Cowper, "is impossible." This, however, is merely an accidental
objection to rhyme. If this were all, it might be
supposed, that if rhymes were more abundant, Homer
could be adequately translated in rhyme. But this
is not so; there is a deeper, a substantial objection
to rhyme in a translation of Homer. It is, that
rhyme inevitably tends to pair lines which in the
original are independent, and thus the movement of
the poem is changed. In these lines of Chapman, for
instance, from Sarpedon's speech to Glaucus, in the
twelfth book of the *Iliad :—*

> "O friend, if keeping back
> Would keep back age from us, and death, and that we might
> not wrack
> In this life's human sea at all, but that deferring now
> We shunned death ever,—nor would I half this vain va or show,
> Nor glorify a folly so, to wish thee to advance ;
> But since we *must* go, though not here, and that besides the
> chance
> Proposed now, there are infinite fates," etc.

Here the necessity of making the line,

> "Nor glorify a folly so, to wish thee to advance,"

rhyme with the line which follows it, entirely changes
and spoils the movement of the passage.

> οὔτε κεν αὐτὸς ἐνὶ πρώτοισι μαχοίμην,
> οὔτε κε σὲ στέλλοιμι μάχην ἐς κυδιάνειραν·[1]
> "Neither would I myself go forth to fight with the foremost,
> Nor would I urge thee on to enter the glorious battle,"

---

[1] *Iliad*, xii. 324.

says Homer; there he stops, and begins an opposed movement :

νῦν δ'—ἔμπης γὰρ Κῆρες ἐφεστᾶσιν θανάτοιο—
"But—for a thousand fates of death stand close to us always"—

This line, in which Homer wishes to go away with the most marked rapidity from the line before, Chapman is forced, by the necessity of rhyming, intimately to connect with the line before.

"But since we *must* go, though not here, and that besides the chance"—

The moment the word *chance* strikes our ear, we are irresistibly carried back to *advance* and to the whole previous line, which, according to Homer's own feeling, we ought to have left behind us entirely, and to be moving farther and farther away from.

Rhyme certainly, by intensifying antithesis, can intensify separation, and this is precisely what Pope does; but this balanced rhetorical antithesis, though very effective, is entirely un-Homeric. And this is what I mean by saying that Pope fails to render Homer, because he does not render his plainness and directness of style and diction. Where Homer marks separation by moving away, Pope marks it by antithesis. No passage could show this better than the passage I have just quoted, on which I will pause for a moment.

Robert Wood, whose *Essay on the Genius of Homer* is mentioned by Goethe as one of the books which fell into his hands when his powers were first developing themselves, and strongly interested him, relates

of this passage a striking story. He says that in
1762, at the end of the Seven Years' War, being
then Under-Secretary of State, he was directed to
wait upon the President of the Council, Lord Granville, a few days before he died, with the preliminary
articles of the Treaty of Paris. "I found him," he
continues, "so languid, that I proposed postponing
my business for another time; but he insisted that
I should stay, saying, it could not prolong his life to
neglect his duty; and repeating the following passage
out of Sarpedon's speech, he dwelled with particular
emphasis on the third line, which recalled to his mind
the distinguishing part he had taken in public affairs:—

ὦ πέπον, εἰ μὲν γὰρ πόλεμον περὶ τόνδε φυγόντε,
αἰεὶ δὴ μέλλοιμεν ἀγήρω τ' ἀθανάτω τε
ἔσσεσθ', οὔτε κεν αὐτὸς ἐνὶ πρώτοισι μαχοίμην,[1]
οὔτε κε σὲ στέλλοιμι μάχην ἐς κυδιάνειραν·
νῦν δ'—ἔμπης γὰρ Κῆρες ἐφεστᾶσιν θανάτοιο
μυρίαι, ἃς οὐκ ἔστι φυγεῖν βροτόν, οὐδ' ὑπαλύξαι—
ἴομεν.

His Lordship repeated the last word several times
with a calm and determinate resignation; and, after a
serious pause of some minutes, he desired to hear the
Treaty read, to which he listened with great attention, and recovered spirits enough to declare the
approbation of a dying statesman (I use his own
words) 'on the most glorious war, and most honour-
able peace, this nation ever saw.'"[2]

[1] These are the words on which Lord Granville "dwelled
with particular emphasis."
[2] Robert Wood, *Essay on the Original Genius and Writings
of Homer*, London, 1775, p. vii.

I quote this story, first, because it is interesting as exhibiting the English aristocracy at its very height of culture, lofty spirit, and greatness, towards the middle of the last century. I quote it, secondly, because it seems to me to illustrate Goethe's saying which I mentioned, that our life, in Homer's view of it, represents a conflict and a hell; and it brings out, too, what there is tonic and fortifying in this doctrine. I quote it, lastly, because it shows that the passage is just one of those in translating which Pope will be at his best, a passage of strong emotion and oratorical movement, not of simple narrative or description.

Pope translates the passage thus :—

> " Could all our care elude the gloomy grave
> Which claims no less the fearful than the brave,
> For lust of fame I should not vainly dare
> In fighting fields, nor urge thy soul to war :
> But since, alas ! ignoble age must come,
> Disease, and death's inexorable doom ;
> The life which others pay, let us bestow,
> And give to fame what we to nature owe."

Nothing could better exhibit Pope's prodigious talent; and nothing, too, could be better in its own way. But, as Bentley said, "You must not call it Homer." One feels that Homer's thought has passed through a literary and rhetorical crucible, and come out highly intellectualised ; come out in a form which strongly impresses us, indeed, but which no longer impresses us in the same way as when it was uttered by Homer. The antithesis of the last two lines—

> " The life which others pay, let us bestow,
> And give to fame what we to nature owe "—

is excellent, and is just suited to Pope's heroic couplet; but neither the antithesis itself, nor the couplet which conveys it, is suited to the feeling or to the movement of the Homeric ἴομεν.

A literary and intellectualised language is, however, in its own way well suited to grand matters; and Pope, with a language of this kind and his own admirable talent, comes off well enough as long as he has passion, or oratory, or a great crisis to deal with. Even here, as I have been pointing out, he does not render Homer; but he and his style are in themselves strong. It is when he comes to level passages, passages of narrative or description, that he and his style are sorely tried, and prove themselves weak. A perfectly plain direct style can of course convey the simplest matter as naturally as the grandest; indeed, it must be harder for it, one would say, to convey a grand matter worthily and nobly, than to convey a common matter, as alone such a matter should be conveyed, plainly and simply. But the style of Rasselas is incomparably better fitted to describe a sage philosophising than a soldier lighting his camp-fire. The style of Pope is not the style of Rasselas; but it is equally a literary style, equally unfitted to describe a simple matter with the plain naturalness of Homer.

Every one knows the passage at the end of the eighth book of the *Iliad*, where the fires of the Trojan encampment are likened to the stars. It is very far from my wish to hold Pope up to ridicule, so I shall not quote the commencement of the passage, which in the original is of great and celebrated beauty, and in translating which Pope has been singularly and notoriously fortunate. But the latter part of the passage, where Homer leaves the stars, and comes to the Trojan fires, treats of the plainest, most matter-of-fact subject possible, and deals with this, as Homer always deals with every subject, in the plainest and most straightforward style. "So many in number, between the ships and the streams of Xanthus, shone forth in front of Troy the fires kindled by the Trojans. There were kindled a thousand fires in the plain; and by each one there sat fifty men in the light of the blazing fire. And the horses, munching white barley and rye, and standing by the chariots, waited for the bright-throned Morning." [1]

In Pope's translation, this plain story becomes the following :—

> " So many flames before proud Ilion blaze,
>   And brighten glimmering Xanthus with their rays ;
>   The long reflections of the distant fires
>   Gleam on the walls, and tremble on the spires.
>   A thousand piles the dusky horrors gild,
>   And shoot a shady lustre o'er the field.
>   Full fifty guards each flaming pile attend,
>   Whose umbered arms, by fits, thick flashes send ;
>   Loud neigh the coursers o'er their heaps of corn,
>   And ardent warriors wait the rising morn."

It is for passages of this sort, which, after all, form the bulk of a narrative poem, that Pope's style is so bad. In elevated passages he is powerful, as Homer is powerful, though not in the same way ; but in

---

[1] *Iliad*, viii. 560.

plain narrative, where Homer is still power and delightful, Pope, by the inherent fault of his style, is in-
effective and out of taste.   Wordsworth says somewhere, that wherever Virgil seems to have composed
" with his eye on the object," Dryden fails to render
him.   Homer invariably composes "with his eye on
the object," whether the object be a moral or a
material one : Pope composes with his eye on his
style, into which he translates his object, whatever
it is.   That, therefore, which Homer conveys to us
immediately, Pope conveys to us through a medium.
He aims at turning Homer's sentiments pointedly and
rhetorically ; at investing Homer's description with
ornament and dignity.   A sentiment may be changed
by being put into a pointed and oratorical form, yet
may still be very effective in that form ; but a description, the moment it takes its eyes off that which
it is to describe, and begins to think of ornamenting
itself, is worthless.

Therefore, I say, the translator of Homer should
penetrate himself with a sense of the plainness and
directness of Homer's style ; of the simplicity with
which Homer's thought is evolved and expressed. He
has Pope's fate before his eyes, to show him what a
divorce may be created even between the most gifted
translator and Homer by an artificial evolution of
thought and a literary cast of style.

Chapman's style is not artificial and literary like
Pope's, nor his movement elaborate and self-retarding
like the Miltonic movement of Cowper.   He is plain-
spoken, fresh, vigorous, and, to a certain degree, rapid ;

and all these are Homeric qualities. I cannot say that I think the movement of his fourteen-syllable line, which has been so much commended, Homeric; but on this point I shall have more to say by and by, when I come to speak of Mr. Newman's metrical exploits. But it is not distinctly anti-Homeric, like the movement of Milton's blank verse; and it has a rapidity of its own. Chapman's diction, too, is generally good, that is, appropriate to Homer; above all, the syntactical character of his style is appropriate. With these merits, what prevents his translation from being a satisfactory version of Homer? Is it merely the want of literal faithfulness to his original, imposed upon him, it is said, by the exigences of rhyme? Has this celebrated version, which has so many advantages, no other and deeper defect than that? Its author is a poet, and a poet, too, of the Elizabethan age; the golden age of English literature as it is called, and on the whole truly called; for, whatever be the defects of Elizabethan literature (and they are great), we have no development of our literature to compare with it for vigour and richness. This age, too, showed what it could do in translating, by producing a master-piece, its version of the Bible.

Chapman's translation has often been praised as eminently Homeric. Keats's fine sonnet in its honour every one knows; but Keats could not read the original, and therefore could not really judge the translation. Coleridge, in praising Chapman's version, says at the same time, "It will give you small idea of Homer." But the grave authority of Mr. Hallam pronounces this translation to be "often exceedingly Homeric;" and its latest editor boldly declares that by what, with a deplorable style, he calls "his own innative Homeric genius," Chapman "has thoroughly identified himself with Homer;" and that "we pardon him even for his digressions, for they are such as we feel Homer himself would have written."

I confess that I can never read twenty lines of Chapman's version without recurring to Bentley's cry, "This is not Homer!" and that from a deeper cause than any unfaithfulness occasioned by the fetters of rhyme.

I said that there were four things which eminently distinguished Homer, and with a sense of which Homer's translator should penetrate himself as fully as possible. One of these four things was, the plainness and directness of Homer's ideas. I have just been speaking of the plainness and directness of his style; but the plainness and directness of the contents of his style, of his ideas themselves, is not less remarkable. But as eminently as Homer is plain, so eminently is the Elizabethan literature in general, and Chapman in particular, fanciful. Steeped in humours and fantasticality up to its very lips, the Elizabethan age, newly arrived at the free use of the human faculties after their long term of bondage, and delighting to exercise them freely, suffers from its own extravagance in this first exercise of them, can hardly bring itself to see an object quietly or to describe it temperately. Happily, in the translation of the Bible, the sacred character of their original in-

spired the translators with such respect that they did
not dare to give the rein to their own fancies in dealing
with it. But, in dealing with works of profane literature, in dealing with poetical works above all, which
highly stimulated them, one may say that the minds
of the Elizabethan translators were *too* active; that
they could not forbear importing so much of their
own, and this of a most peculiar and Elizabethan
character, into their original, that they effaced the
character of the original itself.

Take merely the opening pages to Chapman's translation, the introductory verses, and the dedications.
You will find :—

> "An Anagram of the name of our Dread Prince,
>   My most gracious and sacred Mæcenas,
>   Henry, Prince of Wales,
>   Our Sunn, Heyr, Peace, Life,"—

Henry, son of James the First, to whom the work is
dedicated. Then comes an address,

> "To the sacred Fountain of Princes,
>   Sole Empress of Beauty and Virtue, Anne, Queen
>   Of England," etc.

All the Middle Age, with its grotesqueness, its
conceits, its irrationality, is still in these opening
pages; they by themselves are sufficient to indicate
to us what a gulf divides Chapman from the " clearest-
souled " of poets, from Homer; almost as great a gulf
as that which divides him from Voltaire. Pope has
been sneered at for saying that Chapman writes
"somewhat as one might imagine Homer himself to

have written before he arrived at years of discretion."
But the remark is excellent: Homer expresses himself like a man of adult reason, Chapman like a man
whose reason has not yet cleared itself. For instance,
if Homer had had to say of a poet, that he hoped his
merit was now about to be fully established in the
opinion of good judges, he was as incapable of saying
this as Chapman says it,—"Though truth in her very
nakedness sits in so deep a pit, that from Gades to
Aurora, and Ganges, few eyes can sound her, I hope
yet those few here will so discover and confirm that
the date being out of her darkness in this morning of
our poet, he shall now gird his temples with the sun,"
—I say, Homer was as incapable of saying this in that
manner, as Voltaire himself would have been. Homer,
indeed, has actually an affinity with Voltaire in the
unrivalled clearness and straightforwardness of his
thinking; in the way in which he keeps to one thought
at a time, and puts that thought forth in its complete
natural plainness, instead of being led away from it
by some fancy striking him in connection with it, and
being beguiled to wander off with this fancy till his
original thought, in its natural reality, knows him no
more. What could better show us how gifted a race
was this Greek race? The same member of it has not
only the power of profoundly touching that natural
heart of humanity which it is Voltaire's weakness
that he cannot reach, but can also address the under-
standing with all Voltaire's admirable simplicity and
rationality.

My limits will not allow me to do more than

shortly illustrate, from Chapman's version of the *Iliad*, what I mean when I speak of this vital difference between Homer and an Elizabethan poet in the quality of their thought; between the plain simplicity of the thought of the one, and the curious complexity of the thought of the other. As in Pope's case, I carefully abstain from choosing passages for the express purpose of making Chapman appear ridiculous; Chapman, like Pope, merits in himself all respect, though he too, like Pope, fails to render Homer.

In that tonic speech of Sarpedon, of which I have said so much, Homer, you may remember, has :—

εἰ μὲν γὰρ, πόλεμον περὶ τόνδε φυγόντε,
αἰεὶ δὴ μέλλοιμεν ἀγήρω τ' ἀθανάτω τε
ἔσσεσθ',—

"if indeed, but once *this* battle avoided,
We were for ever to live without growing old and immortal."

Chapman cannot be satisfied with this, but must add a fancy to it :—

"if keeping back
Would keep back age from us, and death, and *that we might
not wrack*
In this life's human sea at all ; "

and so on. Again; in another passage which I have before quoted, where Zeus says to the horses of Peleus,

τί σφῶϊ δόμεν Πηλῆϊ ἄνακτι
θνητῷ ; ὑμεῖς δ' ἐστὸν ἀγήρω τ' ἀθανάτω τε·[1]

"Why gave we you to royal Peleus, to a mortal ? but ye are without old age, and immortal."

---

[1] *Iliad*, xvii. 443.

Chapman sophisticates this into :—

> "Why gave we you t' a mortal king, when immortality
> And *incapacity of age so dignifies your states ?*"

Again ; in the speech of Achilles to his horses, where
Achilles, according to Homer, says simply, "Take
heed that ye bring your master safe back to the host
of the Danaans, in some other sort than the last time,
when the battle is ended," Chapman sophisticates this
into :—

> "*When with blood, for this day's fast observed, revenge shall yield*
> *Our heart satiety,* bring us off.*"

In Hector's famous speech, again, at his parting from
Andromache, Homer makes him say : "Nor does my
own heart so bid me" (to keep safe behind the walls),
"since I have learned to be staunch always, and to
fight among the foremost of the Trojans, busy on
behalf of my father's great glory, and my own."[1]   In
Chapman's hand's this becomes :—

> "The spirit I first did breathe
> Did never teach me that ; much less, since the contempt of death
> Was settled in me, *and my mind knew what a worthy was,*
> *Whose office is to lead in fight, and give no danger pass*
> *Without improvement.   In this fire must Hector's trial shine :*
> *Here must his country, father, friends, be in him made divine.*"

You see how ingeniously Homer's plain thought is
tormented, as the French would say, here.   Homer
goes on : "For well I know this in my mind and in
my heart, the day will be, when sacred Troy shall
perish :"—

> ἔσσεται ἦμαρ, ὅτ᾽ ἄν ποτ᾽ ὀλώλῃ Ἴλιος ἱρή.

---

[1] *Iliad,* vi. 444.

Chapman makes this :—

"And such a *stormy* day shall come, in mind and soul I know,
    When sacred Troy *shall shed her towers, for tears of over-
        throw*."

I might go on for ever, but I could not give you a
better illustration than this last, of what I mean by
saying that the Elizabethan poet fails to render Homer
because he cannot forbear to interpose a play of
thought between his object and its expression. Chapman translates his object into Elizabethan, as Pope
translates it into the Augustan of Queen Anne ; both
convey it to us through a medium. Homer, on the
other hand, sees his object and conveys it to us
immediately.

And yet, in spite of this perfect plainness and
directness of Homer's style, in spite of this perfect
plainness and directness of his ideas, he is eminently
noble ; he works as entirely in the grand style, he is
as grandiose, as Phidias, or Dante, or Michael Angelo.
This is what makes his translators despair. "To give
relief," says Cowper, "to prosaic subjects" (such as
dressing, eating, drinking, harnessing, travelling, going
to bed), that is to treat such subjects nobly, in the
grand style, "without seeming unreasonably tumid,
is extremely difficult." It *is* difficult, but Homer has
done it. Homer is precisely the incomparable poet
he is, because he has done it. His translator must
not be tumid, must not be artificial, must not be
literary ; true : but then also he must not be commonplace, must not be ignob e. I have shown you how
translators of Homer fail by wanting rapidity, by

wanting simplicity of style, by wanting plainness of
thought : in a second lecture I will show you how a
translator fails by wanting nobility.

II.

I must repeat what I said in beginning, that the
translator of Homer ought steadily to keep in mind
where lies the real test of the success of his translation, what judges he is to try to satisfy. He is to
try to satisfy *scholars*, because scholars alone have the
means of really judging him. A scholar may be a
pedant, it is true, and then his judgment will be
worthless; but a scholar may also have poetical feeling, and then he can judge him truly; whereas all
the poetical feeling in the world will not enable a
man who is not a scholar to judge him truly. For
the translator is to reproduce Homer, and the scholar
alone has the means of knowing that Homer who is
to be reproduced. He knows him but imperfectly,
for he is separated from him by time, race, and language; but he alone knows him at all. Yet people
speak as if there were two real tribunals in this
matter,—the scholar's tribunal, and that of the
general public. They speak as if the scholar's judgment was one thing, and the general public's judgment
another; both with their shortcomings, both with
their liability to error; but both to be regarded by
the translator. The translator who makes verbal
literalness his chief care "will," says a writer in the
National Review whom I have already quoted, "be

appreciated by the scholar accustomed to test a translation rigidly by comparison with the original, to look perhaps with excessive care to finish in detail rather than boldness and general effect, and find pardon even for a version that seems bare and bold, so it be scholastic and faithful. But, if the scholar in judging a translation looks to detail rather than to general effect, he judges it pedantically and ill. The appeal, however, lies not from the pedantic scholar to the general public, which can only like or dislike Chapman's version, or Pope's, or Mr. Newman's, but cannot *judge* them; it lies from the pedantic scholar to the scholar who is not pedantic, who knows that Homer is Homer by his general effect, and not by his single words, and who demands but one thing in a translation,—that it shall, as nearly as possible, reproduce for him the *general effect* of Homer. This, then, remains the one proper aim of the translator : to reproduce on the intelligent scholar, as nearly as possible, the general effect of Homer. Except so far as he reproduces this, he loses his labour, even though he may make a spirited *Iliad* of his own, like Pope, or translate Homer's *Iliad* word for word, like Mr. Newman. If his proper aim were to stimulate in any manner possible the general public, he might be right in following Pope's example; if his proper aim were to help schoolboys to construe Homer, he might be right in following Mr. Newman's. But it is not : his proper aim is, I repeat it yet once more, to reproduce on the intelligent scholar, as nearly as he can, the general effect of Homer.

When, therefore, Cowper says, "My chief boast is that I have adhered closely to my original;" when Mr. Newman says, "My aim is to retain every peculiarity of the original, to be *faithful*, exactly as is the case with the draughtsman of the Elgin marbles;" their real judge only replies: "It may be so: reproduce then upon us, reproduce the effect of Homer, as a good copy reproduces the effect of the Elgin marbles."

When, again, Mr. Newman tells us that "by an exhaustive process of argument and experiment" he has found a metre which is at once the metre of "the modern Greek epic," and a metre "like in moral genius" to Homer's metre, his judge has still but the same answer for him: "It may be so; reproduce then on our ear something of the effect produced by the movement of Homer."

But what is the general effect which Homer produces on Mr. Newman himself? because, when we know this, we shall know whether he and his judges are agreed at the outset, whether we may expect him, if he can reproduce the effect he feels, if his hand does not betray him in the execution, to satisfy his judges and to succeed. If, however, Mr. Newman's impression from Homer is something quite different from that of his judges, then it can hardly be expected that any amount of labour or talent will enable him to reproduce for them *their* Homer.

Mr. Newman does not leave us in doubt as to the general effect which Homer makes upon him. As I have told you what is the general effect which Homer makes upon me,—that of a most rapidly moving poet, that of a poet most plain and direct in his style, that of a poet most plain and direct in his ideas, that of a poet eminently noble,—so Mr. Newman tells us his general impression of Homer. "Homer's style," he says, "is direct, popular, forcible, quaint, flowing, garrulous." Again: "Homer rises and sinks with his subject, is prosaic when it is tame, is low when it is mean."

I lay my finger on four words in these two sentences of Mr. Newman, and I say that the man who could apply those words to Homer can never render Homer truly. The four words are these: *quaint, garrulous, prosaic, low*. Search the English language for a word which does not apply to Homer, and you could not fix on a better than *quaint*, unless perhaps you fixed on one of the other three.

Again; "to translate Homer suitably," says Mr. Newman, "we need a diction sufficiently antiquated to obtain pardon of the reader for its frequent homeliness." "I am concerned," he says again, "with the artistic problem of attaining a plausible aspect of moderate antiquity, while remaining easily intelligible." And again, he speaks of "the more antiquated style suited to this subject." Quaint! antiquated!—but to whom? Sir Thomas Browne is quaint, and the diction of Chaucer is antiquated: does Mr. Newman suppose that Homer seemed quaint to Sophocles, when he read him, as Sir Thomas Browne seems quaint to us, when we read him? or that Homer's diction seemed antiquated to Sophocles, as Chaucer's diction seems antiquated to us? But we cannot really know, I confess, how Homer seemed to Sophocles : well then, to those who can tell us how he seems to them, to the living scholar, to our only present witness on this matter,—does Homer make on the Provost of Eton, when he reads him, the impression of a poet quaint and antiquated ? does he make this impression on Professor Thompson, or Professor Jowett ? When Shakspeare says, "The princes *orgulous*," meaning "the proud princes," we say, "This is antiquated;" when he says of the Trojan gates, that they

> "With massy staples
> And corresponsive and fulfilling bolts
> *Sperr* up the sons of Troy,"

we say, "This is both quaint and antiquated." But does Homer ever compose in a language which produces on the scholar at all the same impression as this language which I have quoted from Shakspeare ? Never once. Shakspeare is quaint and antiquated in the lines which I have just quoted; but Shakspeare—need I say it ?—can compose, when he likes, when he is at his best, in a language perfectly simple, perfectly intelligible; in a language which, in spite of the two centuries and a half which part its author from us, stops us or surprises us as little as the language of a contemporary. And Homer has not Shakspeare's variations : Homer always composes as Shakspeare composes at his best; Homer is always simple and intelligible, as Shakspeare is often; Homer is never quaint and antiquated, as Shakspeare is sometimes.

When Mr. Newman says that Homer is garrulous, he seems, perhaps, to depart less widely from the common opinion than when he calls him quaint; for is there not Horace's authority for asserting that "the good Homer sometimes nods," *bonus dormitat Homerus?* and a great many people have come, from the currency of this well-known criticism, to represent Homer to themselves as a diffuse old man, with the full-stocked mind, but also with the occasional slips and weaknesses of old age. Horace has said better things than his "bonus dormitat Homerus;" but he never meant by this, as I need not remind any one who knows the passage, that Homer was garrulous, or anything of the kind. Instead, however, of either discussing what Horace meant, or discussing Homer's garrulity as a general question, I prefer to bring to my mind some style which *is* garrulous, and to ask myself, to ask you, whether anything at all of the impression made by that style is ever made by the style of Homer. The mediæval romancers, for instance, are garrulous; the following, to take out of a thousand instances the first which comes to hand, is in a garrulous manner. It is from the romance of Richard Cœur de Lion.

> "Of my tale be not a-wondered!
> The French says he slew an hundred
> (Whereof is made this English saw)
> Or he rested him any thraw.
> Him followed many an English knight
> That eagerly holp him for to fight,"—

and so on. Now the manner of that composition I call garrulous; every one will feel it to be garrulous;

every one will understand what is meant when it is called garrulous. Then I ask the scholar,—does Homer's manner ever make upon you, I do not say, the same impression of its garrulity as that passage, but does it make, ever for one moment, an impression in the slightest way resembling, in the remotest degree akin to, the impression made by that passage of the mediæval poet? I have no fear of the answer.

I follow the same method with Mr. Newman's two other epithets, *prosaic* and *low*. "Homer rises and sinks with his subject," says Mr. Newman; "is prosaic when it is tame, is low when it is mean." First I say, Homer is never, in any sense, to be with truth called prosaic; he is never to be called low. He does not rise and sink with his subject; on the contrary, his manner invests his subject, whatever his subject be, with nobleness. Then I look for an author of whom it may with truth be said, that he "rises and sinks with its subject, is prosaic when it is tame, is low when it is mean." Defoe is eminently such an author; of Defoe's manner it may with perfect precision be said, that it follows his matter; his lifelike composition takes its character from the facts which it conveys, not from the nobleness of the composer. In *Moll Flanders* and *Colonel Jack*, Defoe is undoubtedly prosaic when his subject is tame, low when his subject is mean. Does Homer's manner in the *Iliad*, I ask the scholar, ever make upon him an impression at all like the impression made by Defoe's manner in *Moll Flanders* and *Colonel Jack*? Does it not, on the contrary, leave him with an impression of nobleness, even when it deals with Thersites or with Irus?

Well then, Homer is neither quaint, nor garrulous, nor prosaic, nor mean : and Mr. Newman, in seeing him so, sees him differently from those who are to judge Mr. Newman's rendering of him. By pointing out how a wrong conception of Homer affects Mr. Newman's translation, I hope to place in still clearer light those four cardinal truths which I pronounce essential for him who would have a right conception of Homer; that Homer is rapid, that he is plain and direct in word and style, that he is plain and direct in his ideas, and that he is noble.

Mr. Newman says that in fixing on a style for suitably rendering Homer, as he conceives him, he "alights on the delicate line which separates the *quaint* from the *grotesque*." "I ought to be quaint," he says, "I ought not to be grotesque." This is a most unfortunate sentence. Mr. Newman is grotesque, which he himself says he ought not to be; and he ought not to be quaint, which he himself says he ought to be.

"No two persons will agree," says Mr. Newman, "as to where the quaint ends and the grotesque begins;" and perhaps this is true. But, in order to avoid all ambiguity in the use of the two words, it is enough to say, that most persons would call an expression which produced on them a very strong sense of its incongruity, and which violently surprised them, *grotesque;* and an expression, which produced on them a slighter sense of its incongruity, and which more

gently surprised them, *quaint*.   Using the two words
in this manner, I say, that when Mr. Newman translates Helen's words to Hector in the sixth book,

Δᾶερ ἐμεῖο, κυνὸς κακομηχάνου, ὀκρυοέσσης,[1]—

"O, brother thou of me, who am a mischief-working vixen,
    A numbing horror,"—

he is grotesque ; that is, he expresses himself in a
manner which produces on us a very strong sense of
its incongruity, and which violently surprises us.   I
say, again, that when Mr. Newman translates the
common line,

Τὴν δ᾽ ἠμείβετ᾽ ἔπειτα μέγας κορυθαίολος Ἕκτωρ,—

"Great Hector of the motley helm then spake to her respon-
    sive,"—

or the common expression ἐϋκνήμιδες Ἀχαιοί, "dapper-
greaved Achaians," he is quaint ; that is, he expresses
himself in a manner which produces on us a slighter
sense of incongruity, and which more gently surprises
us.   But violent and gentle surprise are alike far from
the scholar's spirit when he reads in Homer κυνὸς κακομηχάνου, or, κορυθαίολος Ἕκτωρ, or, ἐϋκνήμιδες Ἀχαιοί.
These expressions no more seem odd to him than the
simplest expressions in English.   He is not more
checked by any feeling of strangeness, strong or weak,
when he reads them, than when he reads in an English book "the painted savage," or, "the phlegmatic
Dutchman."   Mr. Newman's renderings of them must,
therefore, be wrong expressions in a translation of
Homer, because they excite in the scholar, their only

[1] *Iliad*, vi. 344.

competent judge, a feeling quite alien to that excited
in him by what they profess to render.

Mr. Newman, by expressions of this kind, is false
to his original in two ways. He is false to him inasmuch as he is ignoble ; for a noble air, and a grotesque
air, the air of the address,

Δᾶερ ἐμεῖο, κυνὸς κακομηχάνου, ὀκρυοέσσης,—

and the air of the address,

"O, brother thou of me, who am a mischief-working vixen,
A numbing horror,"—

are just contrary the one to the other : and he is false
to him inasmuch as he is odd ; for an odd diction like
Mr. Newman's, and a perfectly plain natural diction
like Homer's,— "dapper-greaved Achaians" and ἐϋκνήμιδες Ἀχαιοί,—are also just contrary the one to the
other.   Where, indeed, Mr. Newman got his diction,
with whom he can have lived, what can be his test of
antiquity and rarity for words, are questions which I
ask myself with bewilderment.   He has prefixed to
his translation a list of what he calls "the more
antiquated or rarer words" which he has used.   In
this list appear, on the one hand, such words as
doughty, grisly, lusty, noisome, ravin, which are familiar,
one would think, to all the world ; on the other hand
such words as *bragly*, meaning, Mr. Newman tells us,
"proudly fine ;" *bulkin*, "a calf ;" *plump*, "a mass ;"
and so on.   "I am concerned," says Mr. Newman,
"with the artistic problem of attaining a plausible
aspect of moderate antiquity, while remaining easily

intelligible." But it seems to me that *lusty* is not antiquated : and that *bragly* is not a word readily understood. That this word, indeed, and *bulkin*, may have "a plausible aspect of moderate antiquity," I admit ; but that they are "easily intelligible," I deny.

Mr. Newman's syntax has, I say it with pleasure, a much more Homeric cast than his vocabulary ; his syntax, the mode in which his thought is evolved, although not the actual words in which it is expressed, seems to me right in its general character, and the best feature of his version. It is not artificial or rhetorical like Cowper's syntax or Pope's : it is simple, direct, and natural, and so far it is like Homer's. It fails, however, just where, from the inherent fault of Mr. Newman's conception of Homer, one might expect it to fail,—it fails in nobleness. It presents the thought in a way which is something more than unconstrained,—over-familiar ; something more than easy,—free and easy. In this respect it is like the movement of Mr. Newman's version, like his rhythm, for this, too, fails, in spite of some good qualities, by not being noble enough ; this, while it avoids the faults of being slow and elaborate, falls into a fault in the opposite direction, and is slip-shod. Homer presents his thought naturally ; but when Mr. Newman has,

"A thousand fires along the plain, *I say*, that night were burning,"—

he presents his thought familiarly ; in a style which may be the genuine style of ballad-poetry, but which is not the style of Homer. Homer moves freely ; but when Mr. Newman has,

"Infatuate ! O that thou wert lord to some other army,"[1]—

he gives himself too much freedom; he leaves us too much to do for his rhythm ourselves, instead of giving to us a rhythm like Homer's, easy indeed, but mastering our ear with a fulness of power which is irresistible.

I said that a certain style might be the genuine style of ballad-poetry, but yet not the style of Homer. The analogy of the ballad is ever present to Mr. Newman's thoughts in considering Homer ; and perhaps nothing has more caused his faults than this analogy,—this popular, but, it is time to say, this erroneous analogy. " The moral qualities of Homer's style," says Mr. Newman, " being like to those of the English ballad, we need a metre of the same genius. Only those metres, which by the very possession of these qualities are liable to degenerate into *doggerel*, are suitable to reproduce the ancient epic." " The style of Homer," he says, in a passage which I have before quoted, " is direct, popular, forcible, quaint, flowing, garrulous : in all these respects it is similar to the old

---

[1] From the reproachful answer of Ulysses to Agamemnon, who had proposed an abandonment of their expedition. This is one of the " tonic " passages of the *Iliad*, so I quote it :—

" Ah, unworthy king, some other inglorious army
Should'st thou command, not rule over *us*, whose portion for ever
Zeus hath made it, from youth right up to age, to be winding
Skeins of grievous wars, till every soul of us perish."

Iliad, xiv. 84.

English ballad." Mr. Newman, I need not say, is by
no means alone in this opinion. "The most really
and truly Homeric of all the creations of the English
muse is," says Mr. Newman's critic in the *National
Review*, "the ballad-poetry of ancient times ; and the
association between metre and subject is one that it
would be true wisdom to preserve." "It is confessed,"
says Chapman's last editor, Mr. Hooper, "that the
fourteen-syllable verse" (that is, a ballad-verse) "is
peculiarly fitting for Homeric translation." And the
editor of Dr. Maginn's clever and popular *Homeric
Ballads* assumes it as one of his author's greatest and
most undisputable merits, that he was "the first who
consciously realised to himself the truth that Greek
ballads can be really represented in English only by
a similar measure."

This proposition that Homer's poetry is *ballad-
poetry*, analogous to the well-known ballad-poetry of
the English and other nations, has a certain small
portion of truth in it, and at one time probably served
a useful purpose, when it was employed to discredit
the artificial and literary manner in which Pope and
his school rendered Homer. But it has been so extravagantly over-used, the mistake which it was useful
in combating has so entirely lost the public favour,
that it is now much more important to insist on the
large part of error contained in it, than to extol its
small part of truth. It is time to say plainly that,
whatever the admirers of our old ballads may think,
the supreme form of epic poetry, the genuine Homeric
mould, is not the form of the Ballad of Lord Bateman.

I have myself shown the broad difference between
Milton's manner and Homer's; but, after a course of
Mr. Newman and Dr. Maginn, I turn round in despera-
tion upon them and upon the balladists who have misled them, and I exclaim: "Compared with you, Milton
is Homer's double; there is, whatever you may think,
ten thousand times more of the real strain of Homer
in,

> 'Blind Thamyris, and blind Mæonides,
>   And Tiresias, and Phineus, prophets old,' —

than in,

> 'Now Christ thee save, thou proud portèr,
>   Now Christ thee save and see,'[1]—

or in,

> "While the tinker did dine, he had plenty of wine."[2]

For Homer is not only rapid in movement, simple
in style, plain in language, natural in thought; he is
also, and above all, *noble*. I have advised the translator not to go into the vexed question of Homer's
identity. Yet I will just remind him that the grand
argument—or rather, not argument, for the matter
affords no data for arguing, but the grand source from
which conviction, as we read the *Iliad*, keeps pressing
in upon us, that there is one poet of the *Iliad*, one
Homer—is precisely this nobleness of the poet, this
grand manner; we feel that the analogy drawn from
other joint compositions does not hold good here,
because those works do not bear, like the *Iliad*, the
magic stamp of a master; and the moment you have

---

[1] From the ballad of *King Estmere*, in Percy's *Reliques of
Ancient English Poetry*, i. 69 (edit. of 1767).

[2] *Reliques*, i. 241.

anything less than a masterwork, the co-operation or
consolidation of several poets becomes possible, for
talent is not uncommon ; the moment you have *much*
less than a masterwork, they become easy, for medio-
crity is everywhere. I can imagine fifty Bradies joined
with as many Tates to make the New Version of the
Psalms. I can imagine several poets having con-
tributed to any one of the old English ballads in
Percy's collection. I can imagine several poets,
possessing, like Chapman, the Elizabethan vigour and
the Elizabethan mannerism, united with Chapman
to produce his version of the *Iliad*. I can imagine
several poets, with the literary knack of the twelfth
century, united to produce the *Nibelungen Lay* in
the form in which we have it,—a work which the
Germans, in their joy at discovering a national epic
of their own, have rated vastly higher than it deserves.
And lastly, though Mr. Newman's translation of Homer
bears the strong mark of his own idiosyncrasy, yet I
can imagine Mr. Newman and a school of adepts
trained by him in his art of poetry, jointly producing
that work, so that Aristarchus himself should have
difficulty in pronouncing which line was the master's,
and which a pupil's. But I cannot imagine several
poets, or one poet, joined with Dante in the composition of his *Inferno*, though many poets have taken
for their subject a descent into Hell. Many artists,
again, have represented Moses ; but there is only one
Moses of Michael Angelo. So the insurmountable
obstacle to believing the *Iliad* a consolidated work of
several poets is this : that the work of great masters

is unique; and the *Iliad* has a great master's genuine stamp, and that stamp is *the grand style.*

Poets who cannot work in the grand style instinctively seek a style in which their comparative inferiority may feel itself at ease, a manner which may be, so to speak, indulgent to their inequalities. The ballad-style offers to an epic poet, quite unable to fill the canvas of Homer, or Dante, or Milton, a canvas which he is capable of filling. The ballad-measure is quite able to give due effect to the vigour and spirit which its employer, when at his very best, may be able to exhibit; and, when he is not at his best, when he is a little trivial, or a little dull, it will not betray him, it will not bring out his weaknesses into broad relief. This is a convenience; but it is a convenience which the ballad-style purchases by resigning all pretensions to the highest, to the grand manner. It is true of its movement, as it is *not* true of Homer's, that it is "liable to degenerate into doggerel." It is true of its "moral qualities," as it is *not* true of Homer's, that "quaintness" and "garrulity" are among them. It is true of its employers, as it is *not* true of Homer, that they "rise and sink with their subject, are prosaic when it is tame, are low when it is mean." For this reason the ballad-style and the ballad-measure are eminently *in*appropriate to render Homer. Homer's manner and movement are always both noble and powerful: the ballad-manner and movement are often either jaunty and smart, so not noble; or jog-trot and humdrum, so not powerful.

The *Nibelungen Lay* affords a good illustration of the qualities of the ballad-manner. Based on grand traditions, which had found expression in a grand lyric poetry, the German epic poem of the *Nibelungen Lay*, though it is interesting, and though it has good passages, is itself anything rather than a grand poem. It is a poem of which the composer is, to speak the truth, a very ordinary mortal, and often, therefore, like other ordinary mortals, very prosy. It is in a measure which eminently adapts itself to this commonplace personality of its composer, which has much the movement of the well-known measures of Tate and Brady, and can jog on, for hundreds of lines at a time, with a level ease which reminds one of Sheridan's saying that easy writing may be often such hard reading. But, instead of occupying myself with the *Nibelungen Lay*, I prefer to look at the ballad-style as directly applied to Homer, in Chapman's version and Mr. Newman's, and in the *Homeric Ballads* of Dr. Maginn.

First I take Chapman. I have already shown that Chapman's conceits are un-Homeric, and that his rhyme is un-Homeric; I will now show how his manner and movement are un-Homeric. Chapman's diction, I have said, is generally good; but it must be called good with this reserve, that, though it has Homer's plainness and directness, it often offends him who knows Homer, by wanting Homer's nobleness. In a passage which I have already quoted, the address of Zeus to the horses of Achilles, where Homer has—

ἇ δειλώ, τί σφῶϊ δόμεν Πηλῆϊ ἄνακτι
θνητῷ ; ὑμεῖς δ' ἐστὸν ἀγήρω τ' ἀθανάτω τε !
ἦ ἵνα δυστήνοισι μετ' ἀνδράσιν ἄλγε' ἔχητον ; [1]

Chapman has—

" ' *Poor wretched beasts*,' said he,
'Why gave we you to a mortal king, when immortality
And incapacity of age so dignifies your states?
Was it to haste[2] the miseries poured out on human fates?' "

There are many faults in this rendering of Chapman's, but what I particularly wish to notice in it is the expression "Poor wretched beasts" for ἇ δειλώ. This expression just illustrates the difference between the ballad-manner and Homer's. The ballad-manner—Chapman's manner—is, I say, pitched sensibly lower than Homer's. The ballad-manner requires that an expression shall be plain and natural, and then it asks no more. Homer's manner requires that an expression shall be plain and natural, but it also requires that it shall be noble. 'A δειλώ is as plain, as simple as "Poor wretched beasts;" but it is also noble, which "Poor wretched beasts" is not. "Poor wretched beasts" is, in truth, a little over-familiar, but this is no objection to it for the ballad-manner; it is good enough for the old English ballad, good enough for the *Nibelungen Lay*, good enough for Chapman's *Iliad*, good enough for Mr. Newman's *Iliad*, good enough for Dr. Maginn's *Homeric Ballads;* but it is not good enough for Homer.

[1] *Iliad*, xvii. 443.
[2] All the editions which I have seen have "haste," but the right reading must certainly be "taste."

To feel that Chapman's measure, though natural, is not Homeric; that, though tolerably rapid, it has not Homer's rapidity; that it has a jogging rapidity rather than a flowing rapidity; and a movement familiar rather than nobly easy, one has only, I think, to read half a dozen lines in any part of his version. I prefer to keep as much as possible to passages which I have already noticed, so I wil. quote the conclusion of the nineteenth book, where Achilles answers his horse Xanthus, who has prophesied his death to him.[1]

> "Achilles, far in rage,
> Thus answered him :—It fits not thee thus proudly to presage
> My overthrow.   I know myself it is my fate to fall
> Thus far from Phthia ; yet that fate shall fail to vent her gall
> Till mine vent thousands.—These words said, he fell to horrid deeds,
> Gave dreadful signal, and forthright made fly his one-hoofed steeds."

For what regards the manner of this passage, the words "Achilles Thus answered him," and "I know myself it is my fate to fall Thus far from Phthia," are in Homer's manner, and all the rest is out of it. But for what regards its movement, who, after being jolted by Chapman through such verse as this,—

> "These words said, he fell to horrid deeds,
> Gave dreadful signal, and forthright made fly his one-hoofed steeds,"—

who does not feel the vital difference of the movement of Homer,—

ἦ ῥα, καὶ ἐν πρώτοις ἰάχων ἔχε μώνυχας ἵππους ?

---

[1] *Iliad*, xix. 419.

To pass from Chapman to Dr. Maginn. His
Homeric Ballads are vigorous and genuine poems
in their own way; they are not one continual
falsetto, like the pinchbeck *Roman Ballads* of Lord
Macaulay; but just because they are ballads in their
manner and movement, just because, to use the words
of his applauding editor, Dr. Maginn has "consciously
realised to himself the truth that Greek ballads can
be really represented in English only by a similar
manner,"—just for this very reason they are not at
all Homeric, they have not the least in the world
the manner of Homer. There is a celebrated inci-
dent in the nineteenth book of the *Odyssey*, the
recognition by the old nurse Eurycleia of a scar on
the leg of her master Ulysses, who has entered his
own hall as an unknown wanderer, and whose feet
she has been set to wash. "Then she came near,"
says Homer, "and began to wash her master; and
straightway she recognised a scar which he had got
in former days from the white tusk of a wild boar,
when he went to Parnassus unto Autolycus and the
sons of Autolycus, his mother's father and brethren."[1]
This, "really represented" by Dr. Maginn, in "a
measure similar" to Homer's, becomes:—

> " And scarcely had she begun to wash
> Ere she was aware of the grisly gash
>   Above his knee that lay.
> It was a wound from a wild-boar's tooth,
> All on Parnassus' slope,
> Where he went to hunt in the days of his youth
> With his mother's sire,"—

---

[1] *Odyssey*, xix. 392.

and so on. That is the true ballad-manner, no one
can deny; "all on Parnassus' slope" is, I was going
to say, the true ballad-slang; but never again shall
I be able to read,

> νίζε δ' ἄρ' ἄσσον ἴουσα ἄναχθ' ἐόν· αὐτίκα δ' ἔγνω
> οὐλήν·

without having the detestable dance of Dr.
Maginn's,—

> " And scarcely had she begun to wash
> Ere she was aware of the grisly gash,"—

jigging in my ears, to spoil the effect of Homer, and
to torture me. To apply that manner and that
rhythm to Homer's incidents, is not to imitate
Homer, but to travesty him.

Lastly I come to Mr. Newman. His rhythm, like
Chapman's and Dr. Maginn's, is a ballad-rhythm, but
with a modification of his own. "Holding it," he
tells us, "as an axiom, that rhyme must be abandoned,"
he found, on abandoning it, "an unpleasant void
until he gave a double ending to the verse." In short,
instead of saying,

> " Good people all with one accord
> Give ear unto my *tale*,"—

Mr. Newman would say,

> "Good people all with one accord
> Give ear unto my *story*."

A recent American writer[1] gravely observes that for

---

[1] Mr. Marsh, in his *Lectures on the English Language*, New
York, 1860, p. 520.

his countrymen this rhythm has a disadvantage in being like the rhythm of the American national air *Yankee Doodle*, and thus provoking ludicrous associations.   *Yankee Doodle* is not our national air : for us Mr. Newman's rhythm has not this disadvantage. He himself gives us several plausible reasons why this rhythm of his really ought to be successful : let us examine how far it *is* successful.

Mr. Newman joins to a bad rhythm so bad a diction that it is difficult to distinguish exactly whether in any given passage it is his words or his measure which produces a total impression of such an unpleasant kind.   But with a little attention we may analyse our total impression, and find the share which each element has in producing it.   To take the passage which I have so often mentioned, Sarpedon's speech to Glaucus.   Mr. Newman translates this as follows :—

"O gentle friend ! if thou and I, from this encounter 'scaping,
   Hereafter might forever be from Eld and Death exempted
   As heavenly gods, not I in sooth would fight among the
       foremost,
   Nor liefly thee would I advance to man-ennobling battle.
   Now,—sith ten thousand shapes of Death do any-gait pur-
       sue us
   Which never mortal may evade, though sly of foot and
       nimble ;—
   Onward ! and glory let us earn, or glory yield to some one.—

"Could all our care elude the gloomy grave
   Which claims no less the fearful than the brave"—

I am not going to quote Pope's version over again, but I must remark in passing, how much more, with

all Pope's radical difference of manner from Homer,
it gives us of the real effect of

εἰ μὲν γὰρ, πόλεμον περὶ τόνδε φυγόντε—

than Mr. Newman's lines. And now, why are Mr.
Newman's lines faulty? They are faulty, first, because, as a matter of diction, the expressions "O
gentle friend," "eld," "in sooth," "liefly," "advance,"
"man-ennobling," "sith," "any-gait," and "sly of
foot," are all bad; some of them worse than others,
but all bad: that is, they all of them as here used
excite in the scholar, their sole judge,—excite, I will
boldly affirm, in Professor Thompson or Professor
Jowett,—a feeling totally different from that excited
in them by the words of Homer which these expressions profess to render. The lines are faulty, secondly,
because, as a matter of rhythm, any and every line
among them has to the ear of the same judges (I
affirm it with equal boldness) a movement as unlike
Homer's movement in the corresponding line as the
single words are unlike Homer's words. Οὔτε κε σὲ
στέλλοιμι μάχην ἐς κυδιάνειραν,—"Nor liefly thee
would I advance to man-ennobling battle;"—for
whose ears do those two rhythms produce impressions
of, to use Mr. Newman's own words, "similar moral
genius?"

I will by no means make search in Mr. Newman's
version for passages likely to raise a laugh; that
search, alas! would be far too easy. I will quote
but one other passage from him, and that a passage
where the diction is comparatively inoffensive, in

order that disapproval of the words may not unfairly heighten disapproval of the rhythm. The end of the nineteenth book, the answer of Achilles to his horse Xanthus, Mr. Newman gives thus :—

> "'Chestnut! why bodest death to me? from thee this was not needed.
>
> Myself right surely know alsó, that 't is my doom to perish,
> From mother and from father dear apart, in Troy ; but never
> Pause will I make of war, until the Trojans be glutted.'
> He spake, and yelling, held afront the single-hoofed horses."

Here Mr. Newman calls Xanthus *Chestnut*, indeed, as he calls Balius *Spotted*, and Padorga *Spry-foot;* which is as if a Frenchman were to call Miss Nightingale *Mdlle. Rossignol*, or Mr. Bright *M. Clair.* And several other expressions, too, —"yelling," "held afront," "single-hoofed,"—leave, to say the very least, much to be desired. Still, for Mr. Newman, the diction of this passage is pure. All the more clearly appears the profound vice of a rhythm, which, with comparatively few faults of words, can leave a sense of such incurable alienation from Homer's manner as, "Myself right surely know alsó that 'tis my doom to perish,—compared with the εὖ νύ τοι οἶδα καὶ αὐτὸς, ὅ μοι μόρος ἐνθάδ' ὀλέσθαι of Homer.

But so deeply seated is the difference between the ballad-manner and Homer's, that even a man of the highest powers, even a man of the greatest vigour of spirit and of true genius,—the Coryphæus of balladists, Sir Walter Scott,—fails with a manner of this kind to produce an effect at all like the effect of Homer. "I am not so rash," declares Mr. Newman, "as to

say that if *freedom* be given to rhyme as in Walter
Scott's poetry,"—Walter Scott, "by far the most
Homeric of our poets," as in another place he calls
him,—"a genius may not arise who will translate
Homer into the melodies of *Marmion*." "The *truly*
classical and the *truly* romantic," says Dr. Maginn,
"are one; the moss-trooping Nestor reappears in the
moss-trooping heroes of Percy's *Reliques;*" and a
description by Scott, which he quotes, he calls
"graphic, and therefore Homeric." He forgets our
fourth axiom,—that Homer is not *only* graphic; he
is also noble, and has the grand style. Human nature
under like circumstances is probably in all ages much
the same; and so far it may be said that "the truly
classical and the truly romantic are one;" but it is
of little use to tell us this, because we know the
human nature of other ages only through the repre-
sentations of them which have come down to us, and
the classical and the romantic modes of representation
are so far from being "one," that they remain eternally
distinct, and have created for us a separation between
the two worlds which they respectively represent.
Therefore to call Nestor the "moss-trooping Nestor"
is absurd, because, though Nestor may possibly have
been much the same sort of man as many a moss-
trooper, he has yet come to us through a mode of
representation so unlike that of Percy's *Reliques*, that,
instead of "reappearing in the moss-trooping heroes"
of these poems, he exists in our imagination as something utterly unlike them, and as belonging to another
world. So the Greeks in Shakspeare's *Troilus and*

Cressida are no longer the Greeks whom we have known in Homer, because they come to us through a mode of representation of the romantic world. But I must not forget Scott.

I suppose that when Scott is in what may be called full ballad swing, no one will hesitate to pronounce his manner neither Homeric nor the grand manner. When he says, for instance,

> " I do not rhyme to that dull elf
> Who cannot image to himself,"[1]

and so on, any scholar will feel that *this* is not Homer's manner. But let us take Scott's poetry at its best; and when it is at its best, it is undoubtedly very good indeed :—

> " Tunstall lies dead upon the field,
> His life-blood stains the spotless shield ;
> Edmund is down,—my life is reft,—
> The Admiral alone is left.
> Let Stanley charge with spur of fire,—
> With Chester charge, and Lancashire,
> Full upon Scotland's central host,
> Or victory and England's lost."[2]

That is, no doubt, as vigorous as possible, as spirited as possible ; it is exceedingly fine poetry. And still I say, it is not in the grand manner, and therefore it is not like Homer's poetry. Now, how shall I make him who doubts this feel that I say true ; that these lines of Scott are essentially neither in Homer's style nor in the grand style ? I may point out to him that the movement of Scott's lines, while it is rapid, is also

[1] *Marmion*, canto vi. 38.   [2] *Marmion*, canto vi. 29.

at the same time what the French call *saccadé*, its
rapidity is "jerky;" whereas Homer's rapidity is a
flowing rapidity. But this is something external and
material; it is but the outward and visible sign of an
inward and spiritual diversity. I may discuss what,
in the abstract, constitutes the grand style; but that
sort of general discussion never much helps our judgment of particular instances. I may say that the
presence or absence of the grand style can only be
spiritually discerned; and this is true, but to plead
this looks like evading the difficulty. My best way
is to take eminent specimens of the grand style, and
to put them side by side with this of Scott. For
example, when Homer says:—

> ἀλλά, φίλος, θάνε καὶ σὺ· τίη ὀλυφύρεαι οὕτως;
> κάτθανε καὶ Πάτροκλος, ὅπερ σέο πολλὸν ἀμείνων,[1]

that is in the grand style. When Virgil says:—

> "Disce, puer, virtutem ex me verumque laborem,
>   Fortunam ex aliis,"[2]

that is in the grand style. When Dante says:—

> "Lascio lo fele, et vo pei dolci pomi
>   Promessi a me per lo verace Duca;
>   Ma fino al centro pria convien ch' io tomi,"[3]

---

[1] "Be content, good friend, die also thou! why lamentest
thou thyself on this wise? Patroclus, too, died, who was a far
better than thou."—*Iliad*, xxi. 106.

[2] "From me, young man, learn nobleness of soul and true
effort: learn success from others."—*Æneid*, xii. 435.

[3] "I leave the gall of bitterness, and I go for the apples of
sweetness promised unto me by my faithful Guide; but far as
the centre it behoves me first to fall."—*Hell*, xvi. 61.

that is in the grand style.   When Milton says :—

> "His form had yet not lost
> All her original brightness, nor appeared
> Less than archangel ruined, and the excess
> Of glory obscured,"[1]

that, finally, is in the grand style.   Now let any one, after repeating to himself these four passages, repeat again the passage of Scott, and he will perceive that there is something in style which the four first have in common, and which the last is without; and this something is precisely the grand manner.   It is no disrespect to Scott to say that he does not attain to this manner in his poetry; to say so, is merely to say that he is not among the five or six supreme poets of the world.   Among these he is not; but, being a man of far greater powers than the ballad-poets, he has tried to give to their instrument a compass and an elevation which it does not naturally possess, in order to enable him to come nearer to the effect of the instrument used by the great epic poets,—an instrument which he felt he could not truly use,— and in this attempt he has but imperfectly succeeded. The poetic style of Scott is—(it becomes necessary to say so when it is proposed to "translate Homer into the melodies of *Marmion*")—it is, tried by the highest standards, a bastard epic style; and that is why, out of his own powerful hands, it has had so little success. It is a less natural, and therefore a less good style, than the original ballad-style; while it shares with the ballad-style the inherent incapacity of rising into

[1] *Paradise Lost*, i. 591.

the grand style, of adequately rendering Homer.
Scott is certainly at his best in his battles. Of Homer
you could not say this; he is not better in his battles
than elsewhere; but even between the battle-pieces
of the two there exists all the difference which there
is between an able work and a masterpiece.

> "Tunstall lies dead upon the field,
>   His life-blood stains the spotless shield:
>   Edmund is down,—my life is reft,—
>   The Admiral alone is left."

—"For not in the hands of Diomede the son of
Tydeus rages the spear, to ward off destruction from
the Danaans; neither as yet have I heard the voice
of the son of Atreus, shouting out of his hated mouth;
but the voice of Hector the slayer of men bursts
round me, as he cheers on the Trojans; and they
with their yellings fill all the plain, overcoming the
Achaians in the battle."—I protest that, to my feeling,
Homer's performance, even through that pale and
far-off shadow of a prose translation, still has a hundred
times more of the grand manner about it, than the
original poetry of Scott.

Well, then, the ballad-manner and the ballad-
measure, whether in the hands of the old ballad
poets, or arranged by Chapman, or arranged by Mr.
Newman, or, even, arranged by Sir Walter Scott,
cannot worthily render Homer. And for one reason:
Homer is plain, so are they; Homer is natural, so are
they; Homer is spirited, so are they; but Homer is
sustainedly noble, and they are not. Homer and they
are both of them natural, and therefore touching and

stirring; but the grand style, which is Homer's, is something more than touching and stirring; it can form the character, it is edifying. The old English balladist may stir Sir Philip Sidney's heart like a trumpet, and this is much : but Homer, but the few artists in the grand style, can do more; they can refine the raw natural man, they can transmute him. So it is not without cause that I say, and say again, to the translator of Homer : "Never for a moment suffer yourself to forget our fourth fundamental proposition, *Homer is noble.*" For it is seen how large a share this nobleness has in producing that general effect of his, which it is the main business of a translator to *re*produce.

I shall have to try your patience yet once more upon this subject, and then my task will be completed. I have shown what the four axioms respecting Homer which I have laid down, exclude, what they bid a translator not to do; I have still to show what they supply, what positive help they can give to the translator in his work. I will even, with their aid, myself try my fortune with some of those passages of Homer which I have already noticed ; not indeed with any confidence that I more than others can succeed in adequately rendering Homer, but in the hope of satisfying competent judges, in the hope of making it clear to the future translator, that I at any rate follow a right method, and that, in coming short, I come short from weakness of execution, not from original vice of design. This is why I have so long occupied myself with Mr. Newman's version ; that, apart from all faults of execution, his original design was wrong, and that he has done us the good service of declaring that design in its naked wrongness. To bad practice he has prefixed the bad theory which made the practice bad; he has given us a false theory in his preface, and he has exemplified the bad effects of that false theory in his translation. It is because his starting-point is so bad that he runs so badly; and to save others from taking so false a starting-point, may be to save them from running so futile a course.

Mr. Newman, indeed, says in his preface, that if any one dislikes his translation, "he has his easy remedy; to keep aloof from it." But Mr. Newman is a writer of considerable and deserved reputation; he is also a Professor of the University of London, an institution which by its position and by its merits acquires every year greater importance. It would be a very grave thing if the authority of so eminent a Professor led his students to misconceive entirely the chief work of the Greek world; that work which, whatever the other works of classical antiquity have to give us, gives it more abundantly than they all. The eccentricity too, the arbitrariness, of which Mr. Newman's conception of Homer offers so signal an example, are not a peculiar failing of Mr. Newman's own; in varying degrees they are the great defect of English intellect, the great blemish of English literature. Our literature of the eighteenth century, the literature of the school of Dryden, Addison, Pope, Johnson, is a long reaction against this eccentricity, this arbitrariness; that reaction perished by its own faults, and its enemies are left once more masters of the field. It is much more likely that any new English version of Homer will have Mr. Newman's faults than Pope's. Our present literature, which is very far, certainly, from having the spirit and power of Elizabethan genius, yet has in its own way these faults, eccentricity and arbitrariness, quite as much as the Elizabethan literature ever had. They are the cause that, while upon none, perhaps, of the modern literatures has so great a sum of force been expended as upon the English literature, at the present hour this literature, regarded not as an object of mere literary interest but as a living intellectual instrument, ranks only third in European effect and importance among the literatures of Europe; it ranks after the literatures of France and Germany. Of these two literatures, as of the intellect of Europe in general, the main effort, for now many years, has been a *critical* effort; the endeavour, in all branches of knowledge, theology, philosophy, history, art, science,—to see the object as in itself it really is. But, owing to the presence in English literature of this eccentric and arbitrary spirit, owing to the strong tendency of English writers to bring to the consideration of their object some individual fancy, almost the last thing for which one would come to English literature is just that very thing which now Europe most desires—*criticism*. It is useful to notice any signal manifestation of those faults, which thus limit and impair the action of our literature. And therefore I have pointed out how widely, in translating Homer, a man even of real ability and learning may go astray, unless he brings to the

study of this clearest of poets one quality in which
our English authors, with all their great gifts, are apt
to be somewhat wanting—simple lucidity of mind.

III.

Homer is rapid in his movement, Homer is plain
in his words and style, Homer is simple in his ideas,
Homer is noble in his manner.   Cowper renders him
ill because he is slow in his movement, and elaborate
in his style ; Pope renders him ill because he is artificial both in his style and in his words ; Chapman
renders him ill because he is fantastic in his ideas ;
Mr. Newman renders him ill because he is odd in his
words and ignoble in his manner.   All four translators diverge from their original at other points
besides those named ; but it is at the points thus
named that their divergence is greatest.   For instance,
Cowper's diction is not as Homer's diction, nor his
nobleness as Homer's nobleness ; but it is in movement and grammatical style that he is most unlike
Homer.   Pope's rapidity is not of the same sort as
Homer's rapidity, nor are his plainness of ideas and
his nobleness as Homer's plainness of ideas and nobleness : but it is in the artificial character of his style
and diction that he is most unlike Homer.   Chapman's movement, words, style, and manner, are often
far enough from resembling Homer's movement,
words, style, and manner ; but it is the fantasticality
of his ideas which puts him farthest from resembling
Homer.   Mr. Newman's movement, grammatical

style, and ideas, are a thousand times in strong contrast with Homer's; still it is by the oddness of his diction and the ignobleness of his manner that he contrasts with Homer the most violently.

Therefore the translator must not say to himself: "Cowper is noble, Pope is rapid, Chapman has a good diction, Mr. Newman has a good cast of sentence; I will avoid Cowper's slowness, Pope's artificiality, Chapman's conceits, Mr. Newman's oddity; I will take Cowper's dignified manner, Pope's impetuous movement, Chapman's vocabulary, Mr. Newman's syntax, and so make a perfect translation of Homer." Undoubtedly in certain points the versions of Chapman, Cowper, Pope, and Mr. Newman, all of them have merit; some of them very high merit, others a lower merit; but even in these points they have none of them precisely the same kind of merit as Homer, and therefore the new translator, even if he can imitate them in their good points, will still not satisfy his judge, the scholar, who asks him for Homer and Homer's kind of merit, or, at least, for as much of them as it is possible to give.

So the translator really has no good model before him for any part of his work, and has to invent everything for himself. He is to be rapid in movement, plain in speech, simple in thought, and noble; and *how* he is to be either rapid, or plain, or simple, or noble, no one yet has shown him. I shall try to-day to establish some practical suggestions which may help the translator of Homer's poetry to comply with the four grand requirements which we make of him.

His version is to be rapid ; and of course, to make a man's poetry rapid, as to make it noble, nothing can serve him so much as to have, in his own nature, rapidity and nobleness. *It is the spirit that quickeneth ;* and no one will so well render Homer's swift-flowing movement as he who has himself something of the swift-moving spirit of Homer. Yet even this is not quite enough. Pope certainly had a quick and darting spirit, as he had, also, real nobleness ; yet Pope does not render the movement of Homer. To render this the translator must have, besides his natural qualifications, an appropriate metre.

I have sufficiently shown why I think all forms of our ballad-metre unsuited to Homer. It seems to me to be beyond question that, for epic poetry, only three metres can seriously claim to be accounted capable of the grand style. Two of these will at once occur to every one,—the ten-syllable, or so-called *heroic*, couplet, and blank verse. I do not add to these the Spenserian stanza, although Dr. Maginn, whose metrical eccentricities I have already criticised, pronounces this stanza the one right measure for a translation of Homer. It is enough to observe, that if Pope's couplet, with the simple system of correspondences that its rhymes introduce, changes the movement of Homer, in which no such correspondences are found, and is therefore a bad measure for a translator of Homer to employ, Spenser's stanza, with its far more intricate system of correspondences, must change Homer's movement far more profoundly, and must therefore be for the translator a far worse

measure than the couplet of Pope. Yet I will say, at
the same time, that the verse of Spenser is more
fluid, slips more easily and quickly along, than the
verse of almost any other English poet.

> " By this the northern wagoner had set
> His seven-fold team behind the steadfast star
> That was in ocean waves yet never wet,
> But firm is fixt, and sendeth light from far
> To all that in the wide deep wandering are." [1]

One cannot but feel that English verse has not often
moved with the fluidity and sweet ease of these lines.
It is possible that it may have been this quality of
Spenser's poetry which made Dr. Maginn think that
the stanza of *The Faery Queen* must be a good measure
for rendering Homer. This it is not : Spenser's verse
is fluid and rapid, no doubt, but there are more ways
than one of being fluid and rapid, and Homer is fluid
and rapid in quite another way than Spenser. Spenser's
manner is no more Homeric than is the manner of
the one modern inheritor of Spenser's beautiful gift,—
the poet, who evidently caught from Spenser his sweet
and easy-slipping movement, and who has exquisitely
employed it ; a Spenserian genius, nay, a genius by
natural endowment richer probably than even Spenser ; that light which shines so unexpected and without fellow in our century, an Elizabethan born too
late, the early lost and admirably gifted Keats.

I say then that there are really but three metres,
—the ten-syllable couplet, blank verse, and a third
metre which I will not yet name, but which is neither

---

[1] *The Faery Queen*, Canto ii. stanza 1.

the Spenserian stanza nor any form of ballad-verse,
—between which, as vehicles for Homer's poetry, the
translator has to make his choice. Every one will at
once remember a thousand passages in which both
the ten-syllable couplet and blank verse prove themselves to have nobleness. Undoubtedly the movement and manner of this,—

> " Still raise for good the supplicating voice,
> But leave to Heaven the measure and the choice,"—

are noble. Undoubtedly, the movement and manner
of this :—

> " High on a throne of royal state, which far
> Outshone the wealth of Ormus and of Ind,"—

are noble also. But the first is in a rhymed metre ; and
the unfitness of a rhymed metre for rendering Homer I
have already shown. I will observe, too, that the fine
couplet which I have quoted comes out of a satire, a
didactic poem; and that it is in didactic poetry that the
ten-syllable couplet has most successfully essayed the
grand style. In narrative poetry this metre has succeeded best when it essayed a sensibly lower style, the
style of Chaucer, for instance; whose narrative manner,
though a very good and sound manner, is certainly
neither the grand manner nor the manner of Homer.

The rhymed ten-syllable couplet being thus ex-
cluded, blank verse offers itself for the translator's
use. The first kind of blank verse which naturally
occurs to us is the blank verse of Milton, which has
been employed, with more or less modification, by
Mr. Cary in translating Dante, by Cowper, and by

Mr. Wright in translating Homer. How noble this
metre is in Milton's hands, how completely it shows
itself capable of the grand, nay, of the grandest, style,
I need not say. To this metre, as used in the *Paradise Lost*, our country owes the glory of having produced one of the only two poetical works in the
grand style which are to be found in the modern
languages ; the Divine comedy of Dante is the other.
England and Italy here stand alone ; Spain, France,
and Germany, have produced great poets, but neither
Calderon, nor Corneille, nor Schiller, nor even Goethe,
has produced a body of poetry in the true grand style,
in the sense in which the style of the body of Homer's
poetry, or Pindar's, or Sophocles's, is grand. But
Dante has, and so has Milton ; and in this respect
Milton possesses a distinction which even Shakspeare,
undoubtedly the supreme poetical power in our literature, does not share with him. Not a tragedy of
Shakspeare but contains passages in the worst of
all styles, the affected style ; and the grand style,
although it may be harsh, or obscure, or cumbrous,
or over-laboured, is never affected. In spite, therefore,
of objections which may justly be urged against the
plan and treatment of the *Paradise Lost*, in spite of
its possessing, certainly, a far less enthralling force of
interest to attract and to carry forward the reader than
the *Iliad* or the *Divine Comedy*, it fully deserves, it can
never lose, its immense reputation ; for, like the *Iliad*
and the *Divine Comedy*, nay, in some respects to a higher
degree than either of them, it is in the grand style.

But the grandeur of Milton is one thing, and the

grandeur of Homer is another. Homer's movement, I have said again and again, is a flowing, a rapid movement; Milton's, on the other hand, is a laboured, a self-retarding movement. In each case, the movement, the metrical cast, corresponds with the mode of evolution of the thought, with the syntactical cast, and is indeed determined by it. Milton charges himself so full with thought, imagination, knowledge, that his style will hardly contain them. He is too full-stored to show us in much detail one conception, one piece of knowledge; he just shows it to us in a pregnant allusive way, and then he presses on to another; and all this fulness, this pressure, this condensation, this self-constraint, enters into his movement, and makes it what it is,—noble, but difficult and austere. Homer is quite different; he says a thing, and says it to the end, and then begins another, while Milton is trying to press a thousand things into one. So that whereas, in reading Milton, you never lose the sense of laborious and condensed fulness, in reading Homer you never lose the sense of flowing and abounding ease. With Milton line runs into line, and all is straitly bound together: with Homer line runs off from line, and all hurries away onward. Homer begins, Μῆνιν ἄειδε, Θεά,—at the second word announcing the proposed action : Miton begins :

"Of man's first disobedience, and the fruit
Of that forbidden tree, whose mortal taste
Brought death into the world, and all our woe,
With loss of Eden, till one greater Man
Restore us, and regain the blissful seat,
Sing, heavenly muse."

So chary of a sentence is he, so resolute not to let it escape him till he has crowded into it all he can, that it is not till the thirty-ninth word in the sentence that he will give us the key to it, the word of action, the verb. Milton says:

> "O for that warning voice, which he, who saw
> The Apocalypse, heard cry in heaven aloud."

He is not satisfied, unless he can tell us, all in one sentence, and without permitting himself to actually mention the name, that the man who had the warning voice was the same man who saw the Apocalypse. Homer would have said, "O for that warning voice, which *John* heard,"—and if it had suited him to say that John also saw the Apocalypse, he would have given us that in another sentence. The effect of this allusive and compressed manner of Milton is, I need not say, often very powerful; and it is an effect which other great poets have often sought to obtain much in the same way: Dante is full of it, Horace is full of it; but wherever it exists, it is always an un-Homeric effect. "The losses of the heavens," says Horace, "fresh moons speedily repair; we, when we have gone down where the pious Æneas, where the rich Tullus and Ancus are,—*pulvis et umbra sumus.*" [1] He never actually says *where* we go to; he only indicates it by saying that it is that place where Æneas, Tullus, and Ancus are. But Homer, when he has to speak of going down to the grave, says, definitely, ἐς Ἠλύσιον πεδίον—ἀθάνατοι πέμψουσιν,[2]—"The immortals shall send thee *to the Elysian plain;*" and it

---

[1] *Odes,* IV. vii. 13.   [2] *Odyssey,* iv. 563.

is not till after he has definitely said this, that he adds, that it is there that the abode of departed worthies is placed : ὅθι ξανθὸς ʹΡαδάμανθυς,—" Where the yellow - haired Rhadamanthus is." Again ; Horace, having to say that punishment sooner or later overtakes crime, says it thus :

> "Raro antecedentem scelestum
> Deseruit pede Pœna claudo."[1]

The thought itself of these lines is familiar enough to Homer and Hesiod ; but neither Homer nor Hesiod, in expressing it, could possibly have so complicated its expression as Horace complicates it, and purposely complicates it, by his use of the word *deseruit*. I say that this complicated evolution of the thought necessarily complicates the movement and rhythm of a poet ; and that the Miltonic blank verse, of course the first model of blank verse which suggests itself to an English translator of Homer, bears the strongest marks of such complication, and is therefore entirely unfit to render Homer.

If blank verse is used in translating Homer, it must be a blank verse of which English poetry, naturally swayed much by Milton's treatment of this metre, offers at present hardly any examples. It must not be Cowper's blank verse, who has studied Milton's pregnant manner with such effect, that, having to say of Mr. Throckmorton that he spares his avenue, although it is the fashion with other people to cut down theirs, he says that Benevolus "reprieves The obso-

[1] *Odes*, III. ii. 31.

lete prolixity of shade." It must not be Mr. Tennyson's blank verse.

> "For all experience is an arch, wherethrough
> Gleams that untravelled world, whose distance fades
> For ever and for ever, as we gaze."

It is no blame to the thought of those lines, which
belongs to another order of ideas than Homer's, but it
is true, that Homer would certainly have said of them,
"It is to consider too curiously to consider so." It
is no blame to their rhythm, which belongs to another
order of movement than Homer's, but it is true that
these three lines by themselves take up nearly as much
time as a whole book of the *Iliad*. No; the blank
verse used in rendering Homer must be a blank verse
of which perhaps the best specimens are to be found
in some of the most rapid passages of Shakspeare's
plays,—a blank verse which does not dovetail its lines
into one another, and which habitually ends its lines
with monosyllables. Such a blank verse might no
doubt be very rapid in its movement, and might perfectly adapt itself to a thought plainly and directly
evolved; and it would be interesting to see it well
applied to Homer. But the translator who determines to use it, must not conceal from himself that
in order to pour Homer into the mould of this metre,
he will have entirely to break him up and melt him
down, with the hope of then successfully composing
him afresh; and this is a process which is full of
risks. It may, no doubt, be the real Homer that
issues new from it; it is not certain beforehand that
it cannot be the real Homer, as it is certain that from

the mould of Pope's couplet or Cowper's Miltonic verse it cannot be the real Homer that will issue; still, the chances of disappointment are great. The result of such an attempt to renovate the old poet may be an Æson: but it may also, and more probably will, be a Pelias.

When I say this, I point to the metre which seems to me to give the translator the best chance of pre-serving the general effect of Homer,—that third metre which I have not yet expressly named, the hexameter. I know all that is said against the use of hexameters in English poetry; but it comes only to this, that, among us, they have not yet been used on any con-siderable scale with success. *Solvitur ambulando:* this is an objection which can best be met by *producing* good English hexameters. And there is no reason in the nature of the English language why it should not adapt itself to hexameters as well as the German language does; nay, the English language, from its greater rapidity, is in itself better suited than the German for them. The hexameter, whether alone or with the pentameter, possesses a movement, an ex-pression, which no metre hitherto in common use amongst us possesses, and which I am convinced English poetry, as our mental wants multiply, will not always be content to forego. Applied to Homer, this metre affords to the translator the immense sup-port of keeping him more nearly than any other metre to Homer's movement; and, since a poet's movement makes so large a part of his general effect, and to re-produce this general effect is at once the translator's indispensable business and so difficult for him, it is a great thing to have this part of your model's general effect already given you in your metre, instead of having to get it entirely for yourself.

These are general considerations; but there are also one or two particular considerations which confirm me in the opinion that for translating Homer into English verse the hexameter should be used. The most successful attempt hitherto made at rendering Homer into English, the attempt in which Homer's general effect has been best retained, is an attempt made in the hexameter measure. It is a version of the famous lines in the third book of the *Iliad*, which end with that mention of Castor and Pollux from which Mr. Ruskin extracts the sentimental consolation already noticed by me. The author is the accomplished Provost of Eton, Dr. Hawtrey; and this performance of his must be my excuse for having taken the liberty to single him out for mention, as one of the natural judges of a translation of Homer, along with Professor Thompson and Professor Jowett, whose connection with Greek literature is official. The passage is short;[1] and Dr.

---

[1] So short, that I quote it entire :—

" Clearly the rest I behold of the dark-eyed sons of Achaia ;
  Known to me well are the faces of all ; their names I remember ;
  Two, two only remain, whom I see not among the commanders,
  Castor fleet in the car,—Polydeukes brave with the cestus,—
  Own dear brethren of mine,—one parent loved us as infants.
  Are they not here in the host, from the shores of loved Lace-
      dæmon,
  Or, though they came with the rest in ships that bound through
      the waters,
  Dare they not enter the fight or stand in the council of Heroes,

Hawtrey's version of it is suffused with a pensive
grace which is, perhaps, rather more Virgilian than
Homeric; still it is the one version of any part of
the *Iliad* which in some degree reproduces for me
the original effect of Homer: it is the best, and it
is in hexameters.

This is one of the particular considerations that

> All for fear of the shame and the taunts my crime has awakened?
>   So said she;—they long since in Earth's soft arms were
>   reposing,
> There, in their own dear land, their Fatherland, Lacedæmon."
>   *English Hexameter Translations;* London, 1847 ; p. 242.

I have changed Dr. Hawtrey's "Kastor," "Lakedaimon,"
back to the familiar "Castor," "Lacedæmon," in obedience to
my own rule that everything *odd* is to be avoided in rendering
Homer, the most natural and least odd of poets. I see Mr.
Newman's critic in the *National Review* urges our generation
to bear with the unnatural effect of these rewritten Greek names,
in the hope that by this means the effect of them may have to
the next generation become natural. For my part, I feel no
disposition to pass all my own life in the wilderness of pedantry,
in order that a posterity which I shall never see may one day
enter an orthographical Canaan ; and, after all, the real question is this : whether our living apprehension of the Greek
world is more checked by meeting in an English book about
the Greeks, names not spelt letter for letter as in the original
Greek, or by meeting names which make us rub our eyes and
call out, "How exceedingly odd !"

The Latin names of the Greek deities raise in most cases the
idea of quite distinct personages from the personages whose idea
is raised by the Greek names. Hera and Juno are actually, to
every scholar's imagination, two different people. So in all
these cases the Latin names must, at any inconvenience, be
abandoned when we are dealing with the Greek world. But I
think it can be in the sensitive imagination of Mr. Grote only,
that "Thucydides" raises the idea of a different man from
Θουκυδίδης.

incline me to prefer the hexameter, for translating Homer, to our established metres. There is another. Most of you, probably, have some knowledge of a poem by Mr. Clough, *The Bothie of Toper-na-fuosich*, a long-vacation pastoral, in hexameters. The general merits of that poem I am not going to discuss; it is a serio-comic poem, and, therefore, of essentially different nature from the *Iliad*. Still in two things it is, more than any other English poem which I can call to mind, like the *Iliad*: in the rapidity of its movement, and the plainness and directness of its style. The thought in this poem is often curious and subtle, and that is not Homeric; the diction is often grotesque, and that is not Homeric. Still, by its rapidity of movement, and plain and direct manner of presenting the thought however curious in itself, this poem, which being as I say a serio-comic poem, has a right to be grotesque, is grotesque *truly*, not, like Mr. Newman's version of the *Iliad*, *falsely*. Mr. Clough's odd epithets, "The grave man nicknamed Adam," "The hairy Aldrich," and so on, grow vitally and appear naturally in their place; while Mr. Newman's "dapper-greaved Achaians," and "motley-helmed Hector," have all the air of being mechanically elaborated and artificially stuck in. Mr. Clough's hexameters are excessively, needlessly rough; still, owing to the native rapidity of this measure, and to the directness of style which so well allies itself with it, his composition produces a sense in the reader which Homer's composition also produces,

and which Homer's translator ought to *re*produce,
—the sense of having, within short limits of time,
a large portion of human life presented to him,
instead of a small portion.

Mr. Clough's hexameters are, as I have just said,
too rough and irregular; and indeed a good model,
on any considerable scale, of this metre, the English
translator will nowhere find. He must not follow
the model offered by Mr. Longfellow in his pleasing
and popular poem of *Evangeline;* for the merit of
the manner and movement of *Evangeline*, when they
are at their best, is to be tenderly elegant; and their
fault, when they are at their worst, is to be lumbering; but Homer's defect is not lumberingness, neither
is tender elegance his excellence. The lumbering
effect of most English hexameters is caused by their
being much too dactylic;[1] the translator must learn
to use spondees freely. Mr. Clough has done this,
but he has not sufficiently observed another rule
which the translator cannot follow too strictly; and
that is, to have no lines which will not, as it is
familiarly said, *read themselves*. This is of the last
importance for rhythms with which the ear of the
English public is not thoroughly acquainted. Lord
Redesdale, in two papers on the subject of Greek
and Roman metres, has some good remarks on the

---

[1] For instance; in a version (I believe, by the late Mr.
Lockhart) of Homer's description of the parting of Hector and
Andromache, there occurs, in the first five lines, but one
spondee besides the necessary spondees in the sixth place; in
the corresponding five lines of Homer there occur ten. See
English Hexameter Translations, 244.

outrageous disregard of quantity in which English verse, trusting to its force of accent, is apt to indulge itself. The predominance of accent in our language is so great, that it would be pedantic not to avail one's self of it; and Lord Redesdale suggests rules which might easily be pushed too far. Still, it is undeniable that in English hexameters we generally force the quantity far too much; we rely on justification by accent with a security which is excessive. But not only do we abuse accent by shortening long syllables and lengthening short ones; we perpetually commit a far worse fault, by requiring the removal of the accent from its natural place to an unnatural one, in order to make our line scan. This is a fault, even when our metre is one which every English reader knows, and when he can see what we want and can correct the rhythm according to our wish; although it is a fault which a great master may sometimes commit knowingly to produce a desired effect, as Milton changes the natural accent on the word *Tirésias* in the line :—

"And Tíresias and Phineus, prophets old ;"

and then it ceases to be a fault, and becomes a beauty. But it is a real fault, when Chapman has :—

"By him the golden-throned Queen slept, the Queen of Deities;"

for in this line, to make it scan, you have to take away the accent from the word *Queen*, on which it naturally falls, and to place it on *throned*, which would naturally be unaccented; and yet, after all, you get

no peculiar effect or beauty of cadence to reward you.
It is a real fault, when Mr Newman has :—

"Infatuate! O that thou wert lord to some other army"—

for here again the reader is required, not for any
special advantage to himself, but simply to save Mr.
Newman trouble, to place the accent on the insignifi-
cant word *wert*, where it has no business whatever.
But it is still a greater fault, when Spenser has (to
take a striking instance) :—

"Wot ye why his mother with a veil hath covered his face?"

for a hexameter; because here not only is the reader
causelessly required to make havoc with the natural
accentuation of the line in order to get it to run as a
hexameter; but also he, in nine cases out of ten, will
be utterly at a loss how to perform the process
required, and the line will remain a mere monster for
him.   I repeat, it is advisable to construct *all* verses
so that by reading them naturally—that is, according
to the sense and legitimate accent,—the reader gets
the right rhythm; but, for English hexameters, that
they be so constructed is indispensable.

If the hexameter best helps the translator to the
Homeric rapidity, what style may best help him to the
Homeric plainness and directness?   It is the merit of
a metre appropriate to your subject, that it in some
degree suggests and carries with itself a style appropriate to the subject; the elaborate and self-retarding
style, which comes so naturally when your metre is
the Miltonic blank verse, does not come naturally
with the hexameter; is, indeed, alien to it.   On the

other hand, the hexameter has a natural dignity
which repels both the jaunty style and the jog-trot
style, to both of which the ballad-measure so easily
lends itself. These are great advantages ; and,
perhaps, it is nearly enough to say to the translator
who uses the hexameter that he cannot too religiously
follow, in style, the inspiration of his metre. He will
find that a loose and idiomatic grammar—a grammar
which follows the essential rather than the formal
logic of the thought—allies itself excellently with the
hexameter ; and that, while this sort of grammar
ensures plainness and naturalness, it by no means
comes short in nobleness. It is difficult to pronounce,
certainly, what is idiomatic in the ancient literature
of a language which, though still spoken, has long
since entirely adopted, as modern Greek has adopted,
modern idioms. Still one may, I think, clearly
perceive that Homer's grammatical style is idiomatic,
—that it may even be called, not improperly, a loose
grammatical style.[1] Examples, however, of what I
mean by a loose grammatical style, will be of more
use to the translator if taken from English poetry
than if taken from Homer. I call it, then, a loose
and idiomatic grammar which Shakspeare uses in the
last line of the following three :—

---

[1] See, for instance, in the *Iliad*, the loose construction of ὅστε,
xvii. 658 ; that of ἴδοιτο, xvii. 681 ; that of οἴτε, xviii. 209 ; and
the elliptical construction at xix. 42, 43 ; also the idiomatic
construction of ἐγὼν ὅδε παρασχεῖν, xix. 140. These instances
are all taken within a range of a thousand lines ; any one may
easily multiply them for himself.

" He's here in double trust :
First, as I am his kinsman and his subject,
Strong both against the deed ; "—

or in this :—

" Wit, *whither wilt ?* "

What Shakspeare means is perfectly clear, clearer,
probably, than if he had said it in a more formal and
regular manner ; but his grammar is loose and idiomatic, because he leaves out the subject of the verb
" wilt " in the second passage quoted, and because, in
the first, a prodigious addition to the sentence has to
be, as we used to say in our old Latin grammar days,
understood, before the word " both " can be properly
parsed.   So, again, Chapman's grammar is loose and
idiomatic where he says,

"Even share hath he that keeps his tent, and *he to field* doth go,"—

because he leaves out, in the second clause, the
relative which in formal writing would be required.
But Chapman here does not lose dignity by this
idiomatic way of expressing himself, any more than
Shakspeare loses it by neglecting to confer on
" both " the blessings of a regular government :
neither loses dignity, but each gives that impression
of a plain, direct, and natural mode of speaking, which
Homer, too, gives, and which it is so important, as I
say, that Homer's translator should succeed in giving.
Cowper calls blank verse " a style further removed
than rhyme from the vernacular idiom, both in the
language itself and in the arrangement of it ; " and
just in proportion as blank verse is removed from the

vernacular idiom, from that idiomatic style which is of all styles the plainest and most natural, blank verse is unsuited to render Homer.

Shakspeare is not only idiomatic in his grammar or style, he is also idiomatic in his words or diction; and here, too, his example is valuable for the translator of Homer. The translator must not, indeed, allow himself all the liberty that Shakspeare allows himself; for Shakspeare sometimes uses expressions which pass perfectly well as he uses them, because Shakspeare thinks so fast and so powerfully, that in reading him we are borne over single words as by a mighty current; but, if our mind were less excited,— and who may rely on exciting our mind like Shakspeare ?—they would check us. "To grunt and sweat under a weary load;"—that does perfectly well where it comes in Shakspeare; but if the translator of Homer, who will hardly have wound our minds up to the pitch at which these words of Hamlet find them, were to employ, when he has to speak of one of Homer's heroes under the load of calamity, this figure of "grunting" and "sweating," we should say, *He Newmanises*, and his diction would offend us. For he is to be noble; and no plea of wishing to be plain and natural can get him excused from being this: only, as he is to be also, like Homer, perfectly simple and free from artificiality, and as the use of idiomatic expressions undoubtedly gives this effect,[1] he should

[1] Our knowledge of Homer's Greek is hardly such as to enable us to pronounce quite confidently what is idiomatic in his diction, and what is not, any more than in his grammar;

be as idiomatic as he can be without ceasing to be noble. Therefore the idiomatic language of Shakspeare—such language as, "prate of his *whereabout;*" "*jump* the life to come;" "the damnation of his *taking-off;*" "his *quietus make* with a bare *bodkin*"—should be carefully observed by the translator of Homer, although in every case he will have to decide for himself whether the use, by him, of Shakspeare's liberty, will or will not clash with his indispensable duty of nobleness. He will find one English book and one only, where, as in the *Iliad* itself, perfect plainness of speech is allied with perfect nobleness; and that book is the Bible. No one could see this more clearly than Pope saw it : "This pure and noble simplicity," he says, "is nowhere in such perfection as in the Scripture and Homer : " yet even with Pope a woman is a "fair," a father is a "sire," and an old man a "reverend sage," and so on through all the phrases of that pseudo-Augustan, and most unbiblical, vocabulary. The Bible, however, is undoubtedly the grand mine of diction for the translator of Homer ; and, if he knows how to discriminate truly between what will suit him and what will not, the Bible may afford him also invaluable lessons of style.

I said that Homer, besides being plain in style and

---

but I seem to myself clearly to recognise an idiomatic stamp in such expressions as τολυπεύειν πολέμους, xiv. 86 ; φάος ἐν νήεσσιν θήῃς, xvi. 94 ; τιν' οἴω ἀσπασίως αὐτῶν γόνυ κάμψειν, xix. 71 ; κλοτοπεύειν, xix. 149 ; and many others. The first-quoted expression, τολυπεύειν ἀργαλέους πολέμους, seems to me to have just about the same degree of freedom as the "*jump* the life to come," or the "*shuffle off* this mortal coil," of Shakspeare.

diction, was plain in the quality of his thought.   It
is possible that a thought may be expressed with
idiomatic plainness, and yet not be in itself a plain
thought.   For example, in Mr. Clough's poem, already
mentioned, the style and diction is almost always
idiomatic and plain, but the thought itself is often of
a quality which is not plain; it is *curious*.   But the
grand instance of the union of idiomatic expression
with curious or difficult thought is in Shakspeare's
poetry.   Such, indeed, is the force and power of
Shakspeare's idiomatic expression, that it gives an
effect of clearness and vividness even to a thought
which is imperfect and incoherent; for instance, when
Hamlet says,—

> "To take arms against a sea of troubles,"—

the figure there is undoubtedly most faulty, it by no
means runs on four legs; but the thing is said so
freely and idiomatically, that it passes.   This, however, is not a point to which I now want to call your
attention; I want you to remark, in Shakspeare and
others, only that which we may directly apply to
Homer.   I say, then, that in Shakspeare the thought
is often, while most idiomatically uttered, nay, while
good and sound in itself, yet of a quality which is
curious and difficult; and that this quality of thought
is something entirely un-Homeric.   For example,
when Lady Macbeth says,—

> "Memory, the warder of the brain,
> Shall be a fume, and the receipt of reason
> A limbeck only,"—

this figure is a perfectly sound and correct figure, no doubt; Mr. Knight even calls it a " happy " figure; but it is a *difficult* figure : Homer would not have used it. Again, when Lady Macbeth says,—

> "When you durst do it, then you were a man ;
> And, to be more than what you were, you would
> Be so much more the man,"—

the thought in the two last of these lines is, when you seize it, a perfectly clear thought, and a fine thought; but it is a *curious* thought : Homer would not have used it. These are favourable instances of the union of plain style and words with a thought not plain in quality; but take stronger instances of this union,—let the thought be not only not plain in quality, but highly fanciful : and you have the Elizabethan conceits ; you have, in spite of idiomatic style and idiomatic diction, everything which is most un-Homeric ; you have such atrocities as this of Chapman :—

> "Fate shall fail to vent her gall
> Till mine vent thousands."

I say, the poets of a nation which has produced such conceit as that, must purify themselves seven times in the fire before they can hope to render Homer. They must expel their nature with a fork, and keep crying to one another night and day : "Homer not only moves rapidly, not only speaks idiomatically; he is, also, *free from fancifulness.*"

So essentially characteristic of Homer is his plainness and naturalness of thought, that to the preservation of this in his own version the translator must without scruple sacrifice, where it is necessary, verbal fidelity to his original, rather than run any risk of producing, by literalness, an odd and unnatural effect. The double epithets so constantly occurring in Homer must be dealt with according to this rule; these epithets come quite naturally in Homer's poetry; in English poetry they, in nine cases out of ten, come, when literally rendered, quite unnaturally. I will not now discuss why this is so, I assume it as an indisputable fact that it is so; that Homer's μερόπων ἀνθρώπων comes to the reader as something perfectly natural, while Mr. Newman's "voice-dividing mortals" comes to him as something perfectly unnatural. Well then, as it is Homer's general effect which we are to reproduce, it is to be false to Homer to be so verbally faithful to him as that we lose this effect: and by the English translator Homer's double epithets must be, in many places, renounced altogether; in all places where they are rendered, rendered by equivalents which come naturally. Instead of rendering Θέτι τανύπεπλε by Mr. Newman's "Thetis trailing-robed," which brings to one's mind long petticoats sweeping a dirty pavement, the translator must render the Greek by English words which come as naturally to us as Milton's words when he says, "Let gorgeous Tragedy With sceptred pall come sweeping by." Instead of rendering μώνυχας ἵππους by Chapman's "one-hoofed steeds," or Mr. Newman's "single-hoofed horses," he must speak of horses in a way which surprises us as little as Shakspeare surprises us when he

says, "Gallop apace, you fiery-footed steeds." Instead
of rendering μελιηδέα θυμόν by "life as honey pleasant," he must characterise life with the simple pathos
of Gray's "warm precincts of the cheerful day." Instead of converting ποῖόν σε ἔπος φύγεν ἕρκος ὀδόντων ;
into the portentous remonstrance, "Betwixt the out-
work of thy teeth what word hath slipt ? " he must
remonstrate in English as straightforward as this of
St. Peter, "Be it far from thee, Lord, this shall not
be unto thee ;" or as this of the disciples, "What
is this that he saith, a little while ? we cannot tell
what he saith." Homer's Greek, in each of the places
quoted, reads as naturally as any of those English
passages : the expression no more calls away the attention from the sense in the Greek than in the
English. But when, in order to render literally in
English one of Homer's double epithets, a strange
unfamiliar adjective is invented, — such as "voice-
dividing" for μέροψs, — an improper share of the
reader's attention is necessarily diverted to this an-
cillary word, to this word which Homer never intended
should receive so much notice ; and a total effect
quite different from Homer's is thus produced. Therefore Mr. Newman, though he does not purposely
import, like Chapman, conceits of his own into the
Iliad, does actually import them ; for the result of
his singular diction is to raise ideas, and odd ideas,
not raised by the corresponding diction in Homer ;
and Chapman himself does no more. Cowper says :
" I have cautiously avoided all terms of new inven-
tion, with an abundance of which persons of more

ingenuity than judgment have not enriched our language but encumbered it;" and this criticism so exactly hits the diction of Mr. Newman, that one is irresistibly led to imagine his present appearance in the flesh to be at least his second.

A translator cannot well have a Homeric rapidity, style, diction, and quality of thought, without at the same time having what is the result of these in Homer, —nobleness. Therefore I do not attempt to lay down any rules for obtaining this effect of nobleness,—the effect, too, of all others the most impalpable, the most irreducible to rule, and which most depends on the individual personality of the artist. So I proceed at once to give you, in conclusion, one or two passages in which I have tried to follow those principles of Homeric translation which I have laid down. I give them, it must be remembered, not as specimens of perfect translation, but as specimens of an attempt to translate Homer on certain principles; specimens which may very aptly illustrate those principles by falling short as well as by succeeding.

I take first a passage of which I have already spoken, the comparison of the Trojan fires to the stars. The first part of that passage is, I have said, of splendid beauty; and to begin with a lame version of that would be the height of imprudence in me. It is the last and more level part with which I shall concern myself. I have already quoted Cowper's version of this part in order to show you how unlike his stiff and Miltonic manner of telling a plain story is to Homer's easy and rapid manner :—

> " So numerous seemed those fires the bank between
>   Of Xanthus, blazing, and the fleet of Greece,
>   In prospect all of Troy "—

I need not continue to the end. I have also quoted
Pope's version of it, to show you how unlike his
ornate and artificial manner is to Homer's plain and
natural manner :

> " So many flames before proud Ilion blaze,
>   And brighten glimmering Xanthus with their rays ;
>   The long reflections of the distant fires
>   Gleam on the walls, and tremble on the spires,"—

and much more of the same kind. I want to show
you that it is possible, in a plain passage of this sort,
to keep Homer's simplicity without being heavy and
dull ; and to keep his dignity without bringing in
pomp and ornament. "As numerous as are the stars
on a clear night," says Homer,

> " So shone forth, in front of Troy, by the bed of Xanthus,
>   Between that and the ships, the Trojans' numerous fires.
>   In the plain there were kindled a thousand fires : by each one
>   There sat fifty men, in the ruddy light of the fire :
>   By their chariots stood the steeds, and champed the white
>   barley
>   While their masters sat by the fire, and waited for Morning."

Here, in order to keep Homer's effect of perfect plainness and directness, I repeat the word "fires" as he
repeats πυρά, without scruple ; although in a more
elaborate and literary style of poetry this recurrence
of the same word would be a fault to be avoided. I
omit the epithet of Morning, and, whereas Homer
says that the steeds "waited for Morning," I prefer
to attribute this expectation of Morning to the master

and not to the horse. Very likely in this particular, as in any other single particular, I may be wrong : what I wish you to remark is my endeavour after absolute plainness of speech, my care to avoid anything which may the least check or surprise the reader, whom Homer does not check or surprise. Homer's lively personal familiarity with war, and with the war-horse as his master's companion, is such that, as it seems to me, his attributing to the one the other's feelings comes to us quite naturally ; but, from a poet without this familiarity, the attribution strikes as a little unnatural ; and therefore, as everything the least unnatural is un-Homeric, I avoid it.

Again, in the address of Zeus to the horses of Achilles, Cowper has :

> " Jove saw their grief with pity, and his brows
> Shaking, within himself thus, pensive, said.
>   ' Ah hapless pair ! wherefore by gift divine
> Were ye to Peleus given, a mortal king,
> Yourselves immortal and from age exempt ? ' "

There is no want of dignity here, as in the versions of Chapman and Mr. Newman, which I have already quoted ; but the whole effect is much too slow. Take Pope :—

> " Nor Jove disdained to cast a pitying look
> While thus relenting to the steeds he spoke.
>   ' Unhappy coursers of immortal strain !
> Exempt from age and deathless now in vain ;
> Did we your race on mortal man bestow
> Only, alas ! to share in mortal woe ? ' "

Here there is no want either of dignity or rapidity, but all is too artificial. " Nor Jove disdained," for instance, is a very artificial and literary way of rendering Homer's words, and so is, "coursers of immortal strain."

Μυρομένω δ' ἄρα τώ γε ἰδὼν, ἐλέησε Κρονίων,—
" And with pity the son of Saturn saw them bewailing,
And he shook his head, and thus addressed his own bosom :—
    'Ah, unhappy pair, to Peleus why did we give you
To a mortal ? but ye are without old age and immortal.
Was it that ye, with man, might have your thousands of
    sorrows ?
For than man, indeed, there breathes no wretcheder creature,
Of all living things, that on earth are breathing and moving.'"

Here I will observe that the use of "own," in the second line, for the last syllable of a dactyl, and the use of "To a," in the fourth, for a complete spondee, though they do not, I think, actually spoil the run of the hexameter, are yet undoubtedly instances of that over-reliance on accent, and too free disregard of quantity, which Lord Redesdale visits with just reprehension.[1]

[1] It must be remembered, however, that, if we disregard quantity too much in constructing English hexameters, we also disregard accent too much in reading Greek hexameters. We read every Greek dactyl so as to make a pure dactyl of it ; but, to a Greek, the accent must have hindered many dactyls from sounding as pure dactyls. When we read αἰόλος ἵππος, for instance, or αἰγιόχοιο, the dactyl in each of these cases is made by us as pure a dactyl as "Tityre," or " dignity ;" but to a Greek it was not so. To him αἰόλος must have been nearly as impure a dactyl as "death-destined" is to us ; and αἰγιόχ nearly as impure as the "dressed his own" of my text. Nor, I think, does this right mode of pronouncing the two words at all spoil the run of the line as a hexameter. The effect of αἰόλλος ἵππος (or something like that), though not *our* effect, is not a disagreeable one. On the other hand, κορυθαιόλος as a paroxytonon, although it has the respectable authority of Liddell and Scott's

I now take two longer passages in order to try my method more fully; but I still keep to passages which have already come under our notice.   I quoted Chapman's version of some passages in the speech of Hector at his parting with Andromache.   One astounding conceit will probably still be in your remembrance,—

"When sacred Troy shall *shed her tow'rs for tears of overthrow,*"—

as a translation of ὅτ' ἄν ποτ' ὀλώλῃ Ἴλιος ἱρή.   I will quote a few lines which may give you, also, the key-note to the Anglo-Augustan manner of rendering this passage and to the Miltonic manner of rendering it. What Mr. Newman's manner of rendering it would be, you can by this time sufficiently imagine for yourselves.   Mr. Wright, —to quote for once from his meritorious version instead of Cowper's, whose strong and weak points are those of Mr. Wright also,—Mr. Wright begins his version of this passage thus :

> " All these thy anxious cares are also mine,
>   Partner beloved ; but how could I endure
>   The scorn of Trojans and their long-robed wives,
>   Should they behold their Hector shrink from war,
>   And act the coward's part ?   Nor doth my soul
>   Prompt the base thought."

Ex pede Herculem : you see just what the manner is.

Lexicon (following Heyne), is certainly wrong; for then the word cannot be pronounced without throwing an accent on the first syllable as well as the third, and μέγας κορρυθαιόλλος Ἕκτωρ would have been to a Greek as intolerable an ending for a hexameter line as " accurst *orphanhood-destined* houses " would be to us.   The best authorities, accordingly, accent κορυθαίολος as a proparoxytonon.

Mr. Sotheby, on the other hand (to take a disciple of
Pope instead of Pope himself), begins thus :

> " ' What moves thee, moves my mind,' brave Hector said,
> 'Yet Troy's upbraiding scorn I deeply dread,
> If, like a slave, where chiefs with chiefs engage,
> The warrior Hector fears the war to wage.
> Not thus my heart inclines.' "

From that specimen, too, you can easily divine what,
with such a manner, will become of the whole passage.
But Homer has neither

> " What moves thee, moves my mind,"—

nor has he

> " All these thy anxious cares are also mine."

> 'Η καὶ ἐμοὶ τάδε πάντα μέλει, γύναι· ἀλλὰ μάλ' αἰνῶς,—

that is what Homer has, that is his style and movement, if one could but catch it. Andromache, as
you know, has been entreating Hector to defend
Troy from within the walls, instead of exposing his
life, and, with his own life, the safety of all those
dearest to him, by fighting in the open plain. Hector
replies :—

> " Woman, I too take thought for this ; but then I bethink me
> What the Trojan men and Trojan women might murmur,
> If like a coward I skulked behind, apart from the battle.
> Nor would my own heart let me ; my heart, which has bid
>   me be valiant
> Always, and always fighting among the first of the Trojans,
> Busy for Priam's fame and my own, in spite of the future.
> For that day will come, my soul is assured of its coming,
> It will come, when sacred Troy shall go to destruction,
> Troy, and warlike Priam too, and the people of Priam.
> And yet not that grief, which then will be, of the Trojans,
> Moves me so much—not Hecuba's grief, nor Priam my father's,

Nor my brethren's, many and brave, who then will be lying
In the bloody dust, beneath the feet of their foemen—
As thy grief, when, in tears, some brazen-coated Achaian
Shall transport thee away, and the day of thy freedom be
    ended.
Then, perhaps, thou shalt work at the loom of another, in
    Argos,
Or bear pails to the well of Messeïs, or Hypereia,
Sorely against thy will, by strong Necessity's order.
And some man may say, as he looks and sees thy tears falling:
See, the wife of Hector, that great pre-eminent captain
Of the horsemen of Troy, in the day they fought for their city.
So some man will say ; and then thy grief will redouble
At thy want of a man like me, to save thee from bondage.
But let me be dead, and the earth be mounded above me,
Ere I hear thy cries, and thy captivity told of."

The main question, whether or no this version
reproduces for him the movement and general effect
of Homer better than other versions[1] of the same
passage, I leave for the judgment of the scholar.
But the particular points, in which the operation of
my own rules is manifested, are as follows.   In the
second line I leave out the epithet of the Trojan
women, ἑλκεσιπέπλους, altogether.   In the sixth line
I put in five words, "in spite of the future," which
are in the original by implication only, and are not
there actually expressed.   This I do, because Homer,
as I have before said, is so remote from one who
reads him in English, that the English translator
must be even plainer, if possible, and more unambigu-
ous than Homer himself ; the connection of meaning

---

[1] Dr. Hawtrey also has translated this passage ; but here, he
has not, I think, been so successful as in his "Helen on the
walls of Troy."

must be even more distinctly marked in the translation than in the original. For in the Greek
language itself there is something which brings one
nearer to Homer, which gives one a clue to his
thought, which makes a hint enough; but in the
English language this sense of nearness, this clue, is
gone; hints are insufficient, everything must be stated
with full distinctness. In the ninth line Homer's
epithet for Priam is ἐυμμλείω,—"armed with good
ashen spear," say the dictionaries; "ashen-speared,"
translates Mr. Newman, following his own rule to
"retain every peculiarity of his original,"—I say, on
the other hand, that ἐυμμελίω has not the effect of a
"peculiarity" in the original, while "ashen-speared"
has the effect of a "peculiarity" in English; and
"warlike" is as marking an equivalent as I dare
give for ἐυμμελίω, for fear of disturbing the balance
of expression in Homer's sentence. In the fourteenth
line, again, I translate χαλκοχιτώνων by "brazen-
coated." Mr. Newman, meaning to be perfectly
literal, translates it by "brazen-cloaked," an expression which comes to the reader oddly and unnaturally,
while Homer's word comes to him quite naturally;
but I venture to go as near to a literal rendering as
"brazen-coated," because a "coat of brass" is familiar
to us all from the Bible, and familiar, too, as distinctly
specified in connection with the wearer. Finally, let
me further illustrate from the twentieth line the
value which I attach, in a question of diction, to the
authority of the Bible. The word "pre-eminent"
occurs in that line; I was a little in doubt whether

that was not too bookish an expression to be used in
rendering Homer, as I can imagine Mr. Newman to
have been a little in doubt whether his "responsively
accosted" for ἀμειβόμενος προσέφη, was not too
bookish an expression. Let us both, I say, consult
our Bibles: Mr. Newman will nowhere find it in his
Bible that David, for instance, "*responsively accosted*
Goliath;" but I do find in mine that "the right
hand of the Lord hath the *pre-eminence;*" and forth-
with I use "pre-eminent," without scruple. My
Bibliolatry is perhaps excessive; and no doubt a
true poetic feeling is the Homeric translator's best
guide in the use of words; but where this feeling
does not exist, or is at fault, I think he cannot do
better than take for a mechanical guide Cruden's
Concordance. To be sure, here as elsewhere, the con-
sulter must know how to consult,—must know how
very slight a variation of word or circumstance makes
the difference between an authority in his favour and
an authority which gives him no countenance at
all; for instance, the "Great simpleton!" (for μέγα
νήπιος) of Mr. Newman, and the "Thou fool!" of the
Bible, are something alike; but "Thou fool!" is very
grand, and "Great simpleton!" is an atrocity. So,
too, Chapman's "Poor wretched beasts" is pitched
many degrees too low; but Shakspeare's "Poor
venomous fool, Be angry and despatch!" is in the
grand style.

One more piece of translation and I have done. I
will take the passage in which both Chapman and
Mr. Newman have already so much excited our

astonishment, the passage at the end of the nineteenth book of the *Iliad*, the dialogue between Achilles and his horse Xanthus, after the death of Patroclus. Achilles begins :—

" ' Xanthus and Balius both, ye far-famed seed of Podarga !
See that ye bring your master home to the host of the Argives
In some other sort than your last, when the battle is ended ;
And not leave him behind, a corpse on the plain, like
    Patroclus.'
    " Then, from beneath the yoke, the fleet horse Xanthus
        addressed him :
Sudden he bowed his head, and all his mane, as he bowed it,
Streamed to the ground by the yoke, escaping from under the
    collar ;
And he was given a voice by the white-armed Goddess Hera.
    " ' Truly, yet this time will we save thee, mighty Achilles !
But thy day of death is at hand ; nor shall *we* be the reason—
No, but the will of heaven, and Fate's invincible power.
For by no slow pace or want of swiftness of ours
Did the Trojans obtain to strip the arms from Patroclus ;
But that prince among Gods, the son of the lovely-haired Leto,
Slew him fighting in front of the fray, and glorified Hector.
But, for us, we vie in speed with the breath of the West-Wind,
Which, men say, is the fleetest of winds ; 't is thou who art
    fated
To lie low in death, by the hand of a God and a Mortal.'
    " Thus far he ; and here his voice was stopped by the Furies.
Then, with a troubled heart, the swift Achilles addressed him :
    " ' Why dost thou prophesy so my death to me, Xanthus ?
        It needs not.
I of myself know well, that here I am destined to perish,
Far from my father and mother dear : for all that I will not
Stay this hand from fight, till the Trojans are utterly routed.'

    " So he spake, and drove with a cry his steeds into battle."

Here the only particular remark which I will make is, that in the fourth and eighth line the grammar is what I call a loose and idiomatic grammar. In writing a regular and literary style, one would in the fourth line have to repeat, before "leave" the words "that ye" from the second line, and to insert the word "do;" and in the eighth line one would not use such an expression as "he was given a voice." But I will make one general remark on the character of my own translations, as I have made so many on that of the translations of others. It is, that over the graver passages there is shed an air somewhat too strenuous and severe, by comparison with that lovely ease and sweetness which Homer, for all his noble and masculine way of thinking, never loses.

Here I stop. I have said so much, because I think that the task of translating Homer into English verse both will be re-attempted, and may be re-attempted successfully. There are great works composed of parts so disparate that one translator is not likely to have the requisite gifts for poetically rendering all of them. Such are the works of Shakspeare, and Goethe's *Faust;* and these it is best to attempt to render in prose only. People praise Tieck and Schlegel's version of Shakspeare: I, for my part, would sooner read Shakspeare in the French prose translation, and that is saying a great deal; but in the German poets' hands Shakspeare so often gets, especially where he is humorous, an air of what the French call *niaiserie !* and can anything be more un-Shakspearian than that? Again; Mr. Hayward's prose translation of the first part of *Faust*—so good that it makes one regret Mr. Hayward should have

abandoned the line of translation for a kind of
literature which is, to say the least, somewhat slight
—is not likely to be surpassed by any translation in
verse. But poems like the *Iliad*, which, in the main,
are in one manner, may hope to find a poetical translator so gifted and so trained as to be able to learn
that one manner, and to reproduce it. Only, the
poet who would reproduce this must cultivate in
himself a Greek virtue by no means common among
the moderns in general, and the English in particular,
—*moderation.* For Homer has not only the English
vigour, he has the Greek grace; and when one
observes the boistering, rollicking way in which his
English admirers—even men of genius, like the late
Professor Wilson—love to talk of Homer and his
poetry, one cannot help feeling that there is no very
deep community of nature between them and the
object of their enthusiasm. "It is very well, my
good friends," I always imagine Homer saying to
them: if he could hear them: "you do me a great
deal of honour, but somehow or other you praise me
too like barbarians." For Homer's grandeur is not
the mixed and turbid grandeur of the great poets of
the north, of the authors of *Othello* and *Faust ;* it is
a perfect, a lovely grandeur. Certainly his poetry
has all the energy and power of the poetry of our
ruder climates; but it has, besides, the pure lines of
an Ionian horizon, the liquid clearness of an Ionian
sky.

LAST WORDS.

"Multi, qui persequuntur me, et tribulant me : a testimoniis non declinavi."

BUFFON, the great French naturalist, imposed on himself the rule of steadily abstaining from all answer to attacks made upon him. " Je n'ai jamais répondu à aucune critique," he said to one of his friends who, on the occasion of a certain criticism, was eager to take up arms in his behalf ; "je n'ai jamais répondu à aucune critique, et je garderai le même silence sur celle-ci." On another occasion, when accused of plagiarism, and pressed by his friends to answer, "Il vaut mieux," he said, "laisser ces mauvaises gens dans l'incertitude." Even when reply to an attack was made successfully, he disapproved of it, he regretted that those he esteemed should make it. Montesquieu, more sensitive to criticism than Buffon, had answered, and successfully answered, an attack made upon his great work, the *Esprit des Lois*, by the *Gazetier Janséniste*. This Jansenist Gazetteer was a periodical of those times,—a periodical such as other times, also, have occasionally seen,—very pretentious, very aggressive, and, when the point to be seized was at all a delicate one, very apt to miss it. " Notwithstanding this example," said Buffon,—who, as well as Montesquieu, had been attacked by the Jansenist Gazetteer,—"notwithstanding this example, I think I may promise my course will be different. I shall not answer a single word."

And to any one who has noticed the baneful effects of controversy, with all its train of personal rivalries and hatreds, on men of letters or men of science ; to any one who has observed how it tends to impair, not only their dignity and repose, but their productive force, their genuine activity ; how it always checks the free play of the spirit, and often ends by stopping it altogether ; it can hardly seem doubtful, that the rule thus imposed on himself by Buffon was a wise one. His own career, indeed, admirably shows the wisdom of it. That career was as glorious as it was serene ; but it owed to its serenity no small part of its glory. The regularity and completeness with which he gradually built up the great work which he had designed, the air of equable majesty which he shed over it, struck powerfully the imagination of his contemporaries, and surrounded Buffon's fame with a peculiar respect and dignity. " He is," said Frederick the Great of him, " the man who has best deserved the great celebrity which he has acquired." And this regularity of production, this equableness of temper, he maintained by his resolute disdain of personal controversy.

Buffon's example seems to me worthy of all imitation, and in my humble way I mean always to follow it. I never have replied, I never will reply, to any literary assailant ; in such encounters tempers are lost, the world laughs, and truth is not served. Least of all should I think of using this Chair as a place from which to carry on such a conflict. But when a learned and estimable man thinks he has reason to complain of language used by me in this Chair,—when he attributes to me intentions and feelings towards him which are far from my heart, I owe him some explanation,—and I am bound, too, to make the explanation as public as the words which gave offence. This is the reason why I revert once more to the subject of translating Homer. But being thus brought back to that subject, and not wishing to occupy you solely with an explanation which, after all, is Mr. Newman's affair and mine, not the public's, I shall take the opportunity,—not certainly to enter into any conflict with any one,—but to try to establish our old friend, the coming translator of Homer, yet a little firmer in the positions which I hope we have now secured for him; to protect him against the danger of relaxing, in the confusion of dispute, his attention to those matters which alone I consider important for him; to save him from losing sight, in the dust of the attacks delivered over it, of the real body of Patroclus. He will, probably, when he arrives, requite my solicitude very ill, and be in haste to disown his benefactor; but my interest in him is so sincere that I can disregard his probable ingratitude.

First, however, for the explanation. Mr. Newman has published a reply to the remarks which I made on his translation of the *Iliad*. He seems to think that the respect which at the outset of those remarks I professed for him must have been professed ironically; he says that I use "forms of attack against him which he does not know how to characterise;" that I

" speak scornfully " of him, treat him with " gratuitous insult, gratuitous rancour ; " that I " propagate
slanders " against him, that I wish to " damage him
with my readers," to " stimulate my readers to despise " him.   He is entirely mistaken.   I respect Mr.
Newman sincerely ; I respect him as one of the few
learned men we have, one of the few who love learning for its own sake ; this respect for him I had before
I read his translation of the *Iliad*, I retained it while
I was commenting on that translation, I have not lost
it after reading his reply.   Any vivacities of expression which may have given him pain I sincerely
regret, and can only assure him that I used them
without a thought of insult or rancour.   When I took
the liberty of creating the verb *to Newmanise*, my intentions were no more rancorous than if I had said to
Miltonise ; when I exclaimed, in my astonishment at
his vocabulary, " With whom can Mr. Newman have
lived ? " I meant merely to convey, in a familiar
form of speech, the sense of bewilderment one has at
finding a person to whom words one thought all the
world knew seem strange, and words one thought
entirely strange, intelligible.   Yet this simple expression of my bewilderment Mr. Newman construes into
an accusation that he is " often guilty of keeping low
company," and says that I shall " never want a stone
to throw at him."   And what is stranger still, one of
his friends gravely tells me that Mr. Newman " lived
with the fellows of Balliol."   As if that made Mr.
Newman's glossary less inexplicable to me !   As if he
could have got his glossary from the fellows of Balliol!

As if I could believe that the members of that distinguished society—of whose discourse, not so many
years afterwards, I myself was an unworthy hearer—
were in Mr. Newman's time so far removed from the
Attic purity of speech which we all of us admired,
that when one of them called a calf a *bulkin*, the rest
"easily understood" him; or, when he wanted to
say that a newspaper-article was "proudly fine," it
mattered little whether he said it was that or *bragly !*
No; his having lived with the fellows of Balliol does
not explain Mr. Newman's glossary to me. I will no
longer ask "with whom he can have lived," since
that gives him offence; but I must still declare that
where he got his test of rarity or intelligibility for
words is a mystery to me.

That, however, does not prevent me from enter-
taining a very sincere respect for Mr. Newman, and
since he doubts it, I am glad to reiterate my expression of it. But the truth of the matter is this: I
unfeignedly admire Mr. Newman's ability and learning; but I think in his translation of Homer he has
employed that ability and learning quite amiss. I
think he has chosen quite the wrong field for turning
his ability and learning to account. I think that in
England, partly from the want of an Academy, partly
from a national habit of intellect to which that want
of an Academy is itself due, there exists too little of
what I may call a public force of correct literary
opinion, possessing within certain limits a clear sense
of what is right and wrong, sound and unsound, and
sharply recalling men of ability and learning from any

flagrant misdirection of these their advantages.   I
think, even, that in our country a powerful misdirection of this kind is often more likely to subjugate and
pervert opinion than to be checked and corrected
by it.[1]   Hence a chaos of false tendencies, wasted
efforts, impotent conclusions, works which ought
never to have been undertaken.   Any one who can
introduce a little order into this chaos by establishing
in any quarter a single sound rule of criticism, a
single rule which clearly marks what is right as right,
and what is wrong as wrong, does a good deed; and
his deed is so much the better the greater force he
counteracts of learning and ability applied to thicken
the chaos.   Of course no one can be sure that he has
fixed any such rules; he can only do his best to fix
them; but somewhere or other, in the literary opinion
of Europe, if not in the literary opinion of one nation,
in fifty years, if not in five, there is a final judgment
on these matters, and the critic's work will at last
stand or fall by its true merits.

Meanwhile, the charge of having in one instance
misapplied his powers, of having once followed a false
tendency, is no such grievous charge to bring against

[1] "It is the fact, that scholars of fastidious refinement, but
of a judgment which I think far more masculine than Mr.
Arnold's, have passed a most encouraging sentence on large
specimens of my translation.   I at present count eight such
names."— "Before venturing to print, I sought to ascertain
how unlearned women and children would accept my verses.   I
could boast how children and half-educated women have ex-
tolled them, how greedily a working man has inquired for them,
without knowing who was the translator."—Mr. NEWMAN'S
Reply, pp. 2, 12, 13.

a man ; it does not exclude a great respect for himself personally, or for his powers in the happier manifestation of them. False tendency is, I have said, an evil to which the artist or the man of letters in England is peculiarly prone ; but everywhere in our time he is liable to it,—the greatest as well as the humblest. "The first beginnings of my *Wilhelm Meister*," says Goethe, "arose out of an obscure sense of the great truth that man will often attempt something for which nature has denied him the proper powers, will undertake and practise something in which he cannot become skilled. An inward feeling warns him to desist" (yes, but there are, unhappily, cases of absolute judicial blindness !), "nevertheless he cannot get clear in himself about it, and is driven along a false road to a false goal, without knowing how it is with him. To this we may refer everything which goes by the name of false tendency, dilettanteism, and so on. A great many men waste in this way the fairest portion of their lives, and fall at last into wonderful delusion." Yet after all,—Goethe adds,—it sometimes happens that even on this false road a man finds, not indeed that which he sought, but something which is good and useful for him ; "like Saul, the son of Kish, who went forth to look for his father's asses, and found a kingdom." And thus false tendency as well as true, vain effort as well as fruitful, go together to produce that great movement of life, to present that immense and magic spectacle of human affairs, which from boyhood to old age fascinates the gaze of every man of imagination, and which would be his terror, if it were not at the same time his delight.

So Mr. Newman may see how wide-spread a danger it is, to which he has, as I think, in setting himself to translate Homer, fallen a prey. He may be well satisfied if he can escape from it by paying it the tribute of a single work only. He may judge how unlikely it is that I should "despise" him for once falling a prey to it. I know far too well how exposed to it we all are ; how exposed to it I myself am. At this very moment, for example, I am fresh from reading Mr. Newman's Reply to my Lectures, a reply full of that erudition in which (as I am so often and so good-naturedly reminded, but indeed I know it without being reminded) Mr. Newman is immeasurably my superior. Well, the demon that pushes us all to our ruin is even now prompting me to follow Mr. Newman into a discussion about the digamma, and I know not what providence holds me back. And some day, I have no doubt, I shall lecture on the language of the Berbers, and give him his entire revenge.

But Mr. Newman does not confine himself to complaints on his own behalf, he complains on Homer's behalf too. He says that my "statements about Greek literature are against the most notorious and elementary fact ;" that I "do a public wrong to literature by publishing them ;" and that the Professors to whom I appealed in my three Lectures, "would only lose credit if they sanctioned the use I make of their names." He does these eminent men the kindness of adding, however, that "whether they are pleased with this parading of their names in behalf of paradoxical error, he may well doubt," and that "until they endorse it themselves, he shall treat my process as a piece of forgery." He proceeds to discuss my statements at great length, and with an erudition and ingenuity which nobody can admire more than I do. And he ends by saying that my ignorance is great.

Alas! that is very true. Much as Mr. Newman was mistaken when he talked of my rancour, he is entirely right when he talks of my ignorance. And yet, perverse as it seems to say so, I sometimes find myself wishing, when dealing with these matters of poetical criticism, that my ignorance were even greater than it is. To handle these matters properly there is needed a poise so perfect that the least overweight in any direction tends to destroy the balance. Temper destroys it, a crotchet destroys it, even erudition may destroy it. To press to the sense of the thing itself with which one is dealing, not to go off on some collateral issue about the thing, is the hardest matter in the world. The "thing itself" with which one is here dealing,—the critical perception of poetic truth, —is of all things the most volatile, elusive, and evanescent; by even pressing too impetuously after it, one runs the risk of losing it. The critic of poetry should have the finest tact, the nicest moderation, the most free, flexible, and elastic spirit imaginable; he should be indeed the "ondoyant et divers," the *undulating and diverse* being of Montaigne. The less he can deal with his object simply and freely, the more things he

has to take into account in dealing with it,—the more,
in short, he has to encumber himself,—so much the
greater force of spirit he needs to retain his elasticity.
But one cannot exactly have this greater force by
wishing for it; so, for the force of spirit one has, the
load put upon it is often heavier than it will well
bear. The late Duke of Wellington said of a certain
peer that "it was a great pity his education had been
so far too much for his abilities." In like manner,
one often sees erudition out of all proportion to its
owner's critical faculty. Little as I know, therefore,
I am always apprehensive, in dealing with poetry,
lest even that little should prove "too much for my
abilities."

With this consciousness of my own lack of learning,
—nay, with this sort of acquiescence in it, with this
belief that for the labourer in the field of poetical
criticism learning has its disadvantages,—I am not
likely to dispute with Mr. Newman about matters of
erudition. All that he says on these matters in his
Reply I read with great interest: in general I agree
with him; but only, I am sorry to say, up to a certain point. Like all learned men, accustomed to desire
definite rules, he draws his conclusions too absolutely;
he wants to include too much under his rules; he does
not quite perceive that in poetical criticism the shade,
the fine distinction, is everything; and that, when he
has once missed this, in all he says he is in truth but
beating the air. For instance: because I think Homer
noble, he imagines I must think him elegant; and in
fact he says in plain words that I do think him so,—

that to me Homer seems "pervadingly elegant." But he does not. Virgil is elegant,—"pervadingly elegant,"—even in passages of the highest emotion :

> "O, ubi campi,
> Spercheosque, et virginibus bacchata Lacænis
> Taygeta ! "[1]

Even there Virgil, though of a divine elegance, is still elegant : but Homer is not elegant ; the word is quite a wrong one to apply to him, and Mr. Newman is quite right in blaming any one he finds so applying it. Again ; arguing against my assertion that Homer is not quaint, he says : "It is quaint to call waves *wet*, milk *white*, blood *dusky*, horses *single-hoofed*, words *winged*, Vulcan *Lobfoot* (Κυλλοποδίων), a spear *longshadowy*," and so on. I find I know not how many distinctions to draw here. I do not think it quaint to call waves *wet*, or milk *white*, or words *winged ;* but I do think it quaint to call horses *single-hoofed*, or Vulcan *Lobfoot*, or a spear *longshadowy*. As to calling blood *dusky*, I do not feel quite sure ; I will tell Mr. Newman my opinion when I see the passage in which he calls it so. But then, again, because it is quaint to call Vulcan *Lobfoot*, I cannot admit that it was quaint to call him Κυλλοποδίων ; nor that, because it is quaint to call a spear *longshadowy*, it was quaint to call it δολιχόσκιον. Here Mr. Newman's erudition misleads him : he knows the literal value of the Greek so well, that he thinks his literal rendering

---

[1] " O for the fields of Thessaly and the streams of Spercheios ! O for the hills alive with the dances of the Laconian maidens, the hills of Taygetus ! "—*Georgics*, ii. 486.

identical with the Greek, and that the Greek must
stand or fall along with his rendering.   But the real
question is, not whether he has given us, so to speak,
full change for the Greek, but *how* he gives us our
change : we want it in gold, and he gives it us in
copper.   Again : " It is quaint," says Mr. Newman,
" to address a young friend as ' O Pippin ! '—it is
quaint to compare Ajax to an ass whom boys are
belabouring."   Here, too, Mr. Newman goes much
too fast, and his category of quaintness is too compre-
hensive.   To address a young friend as " O Pippin ! "
is, I cordially agree with him, very quaint ; although
I do not think it was quaint in Sarpedon to address
Glaucus as ὦ πέπον : but in comparing, whether in
Greek or in English, Ajax to an ass whom boys are
belabouring, I do not see that there is of necessity
anything quaint at all.   Again ; because I said that
eld, lief, in sooth, and other words, are, as Mr. Newman
uses them in certain places, bad words, he imagines
that I must mean to stamp these words with an absolute reprobation ; and because I said that " my
Bibliolatry is excessive," he imagines that I brand all
words as ignoble which are not in the Bible.   Nothing
of the kind : there are no such absolute rules to be
laid down in these matters.   The Bible vocabulary is
to be used as an assistance, not as an authority.   Of
the words which, placed where Mr. Newman places
them, I have called bad words, every one may be
excellent in some other place.   Take *eld*, for instance :
when Shakspeare, reproaching man with the depend-
ence in which his youth is passed, says :

> "all thy blessed youth
> Becomes as aged, and doth beg the alms
> Of palsied *eld*," . . .

it seems to me that *eld* comes in excellently there, in a passage of curious meditation; but when Mr. Newman renders ἀγήρω τ' ἀθανάτω τε by "from *Eld* and Death exempted," it seems to me he infuses a tinge of quaintness into the transparent simplicity of Homer's expression, and so I call *eld* a bad word in that place.

Once more. Mr. Newman lays it down as a general rule that "many of Homer's energetic descriptions are expressed in coarse physical words." He goes on: "I give one illustration,—Τρῶες προὔτυψαν ἀολλέες. Cowper, misled by the *ignis fatuus* of 'stateliness,' renders it absurdly:

> 'The powers of Ilium gave the first assault
> Embattled close;'

but it is, strictly, 'The Trojans *knocked forward* (or, thumped, butted forward) *in close pack.*' The verb is too coarse for later polished prose, and even the adjective is very strong (*packed together*). I believe, that 'forward in pack the Trojans pitched,' would not be really unfaithful to the Homeric colour; and I maintain, that 'forward in mass the Trojans pitched,' would be an irreprovable rendering." He actually gives us all that as if it were a piece of scientific deduction; and as if, at the end, he had arrived at an incontrovertible conclusion. But, in truth, one cannot settle these matters quite in this way. Mr. Newman's general rule may be true or false (I dislike to

meddle with general rules), but every part in what
follows must stand or fall by itself, and its soundness
or unsoundness has nothing at all to do with the
truth or falsehood of Mr. Newman's general rule.
He first gives, as a strict rendering of the Greek,
"The Trojans knocked forward (or, thumped, butted
forward), in close pack." I need not say that, as a
"strict rendering of the Greek," this is good,—all
Mr. Newman's "strict renderings of the Greek" are
sure to be, as such, good; but "in close pack," for
ἀολλέες, seems to me to be what Mr. Newman's renderings are not always,—an excellent *poetical rendering* of the Greek; a thousand times better, certainly,
than Cowper's "embattled close." Well, but Mr.
Newman goes on : "I believe that, 'forward in pack
the Trojans pitched,' would not be really unfaithful
to the Homeric colour." Here, I say, the Homeric
colour is half washed out of Mr. Newman's happy
rendering of ἀολλέες; while in "pitched" for προ-
ύτυψαν, the literal fidelity of the first rendering is gone,
while certainly no Homeric colour has come in its
place. Finally, Mr. Newman concludes : "I maintain that 'forward in mass the Trojans pitched,'
would be an irreprovable rendering." Here, in what
Mr. Newman fancies his final moment of triumph,
Homeric colour and literal fidelity have alike abandoned him altogether ; the last stage of his translation
is much worse than the second, and immeasurably
worse than the first.

All this to show that a looser, easier method than
Mr. Newman's must be taken, if we are to arrive at

any good result in these questions. I now go on to follow Mr. Newman a little further, not at all as wishing to dispute with him, but as seeking (and this is the true fruit we may gather from criticisms upon us) to gain hints from him for the establishment of some useful truth about our subject, even when I think him wrong. I still retain, I confess, my conviction that Homer's characteristic qualities are rapidity of movement, plainness of words and style, simplicity and directness of ideas, and, above all, nobleness, the grand manner. Whenever Mr. Newman drops a word, awakens a train of thought, which leads me to see any of these characteristics more clearly, I am grateful to him; and one or two suggestions of this kind which he affords, are all that now,—having expressed my sorrow that he should have misconceived my feelings towards him, and pointed out what I think the vice of his method of criticism,—I have to notice in his Reply.

Such a suggestion I find in Mr. Newman's remarks on my assertion that the translator of Homer must not adopt a quaint and antiquated style in rendering him, because the impression which Homer makes upon the living scholar is not that of a poet quaint and antiquated, but that of a poet perfectly simple, perfectly intelligible. I added that we cannot, I confess, really know how Homer seemed to Sophocles, but that it is impossible to me to believe that he seemed to him quaint and antiquated. Mr. Newman asserts, on the other hand, that I am absurdly wrong here; that Homer seemed "out and out" quaint and antiquated to the Athenians; that "every sentence of him was more or less antiquated to Sophocles, who could no more help feeling at every instant the foreign and antiquated character of the poetry than an Englishman can help feeling the same in reading Burns's poems." And not only does Mr. Newman say this, but he has managed thoroughly to convince some of his readers of it. "Homer's Greek," says one of them, "certainly seemed antiquated to the historical times of Greece. Mr. Newman, taking a far broader historical and philological view than Mr. Arnold, stoutly maintains that it did seem so." And another says: "Doubtless Homer's dialect and diction were as hard and obscure to a later Attic Greek as Chaucer to an Englishman of our day."

Mr. Newman goes on to say, that not only was Homer antiquated relatively to Pericles, but he is antiquated to the living scholar; and, indeed, is in himself "absolutely antique, being the poet of a barbarian age." He tells us of his "inexhaustible quaintnesses," of his "very eccentric diction;" and he infers, of course, that he is perfectly right in rendering him in a quaint and antiquated style.

Now this question,—whether or no Homer seemed quaint and antiquated to Sophocles,—I call a delightful question to raise. It is not a barren verbal dispute; it is a question "drenched in matter," to use an expression of Bacon; a question full of flesh and blood, and of which the scrutiny, though I still think we cannot settle it absolutely, may yet give us a directly useful result. To scrutinise it may lead us

to see more clearly what sort of a style a modern
translator of Homer ought to adopt.

Homer's verses were some of the first words which
a young Athenian heard. He heard them from his
mother or his nurse before he went to school; and at
school, when he went there, he was constantly occupied with them. So much did he hear of them that
Socrates proposes, in the interests of morality, to
have selections from Homer made, and placed in the
hands of mothers and nurses, in his model republic;
in order that, of an author with whom they were
sure to be so perpetually conversant, the young might
learn only those parts which might do them good.
His language was as familiar to Sophocles, we may
be quite sure, as the language of the Bible is to us.

Nay, more. Homer's language was not, of course,
in the time of Sophocles, the spoken or written language of ordinary life, any more than the language of
the Bible, any more than the language of poetry, is
with us; but for one great species of composition—
epic poetry—it was still the current language; it was
the language in which every one who made that sort
of poetry composed. Every one at Athens who
dabbled in epic poetry, not only understood Homer's
language,—he possessed it. He possessed it as every
one who dabbles in poetry with us, possesses what
may be called the poetical vocabulary, as distinguished from the vocabulary of common speech and
of modern prose: I mean, such expressions as *per-
chance* for *perhaps*, *spake* for *spoke*, *aye* for *ever*, *don* for
put on, *charmèd* for *charm'd*, and thousands of others.

I might go to Burns and Chaucer, and, taking
words and passages from them, ask if they afforded
any parallel to a language so familiar and so possessed. But this I will not do, for Mr. Newman
himself supplies me with what he thinks a fair
parallel, in its effect upon us, to the language of
Homer in its effect upon Sophocles. He says that
such words as *mon, londis, libbard, withouten, muchel,*
give us a tolerable but incomplete notion of this
parallel; and he finally exhibits the parallel in all
its clearness, by this poetical specimen :—

> " Dat mon, quhich hauldeth Kyngis af
>   Londis yn féo, niver
> (I tell 'e) feereth aught ; sith hee
>   Doth hauld hys londis yver."

Now, does Mr. Newman really think that Sophocles
could, as he says, "no more help feeling at every
instant the foreign and antiquated character of
Homer, than an Englishman can help feeling the
same in hearing" these lines ? Is he quite sure of
it ? He says he is ; he will not allow of any doubt
or hesitation in the matter. I had confessed we
could not really know how Homer seemed to
Sophocles ;—"Let Mr. Arnold confess for himself,"
cries Mr. Newman, "and not for me, who know
perfectly well." And this is what he knows !

Mr. Newman says, however, that I "play falla-
ciously on the words familiar and unfamiliar;" that
"Homer's words may have been familiar to the
Athenians (*i.e.* often heard) even when they were
either not understood by them or else, being under-

stood, were yet felt and known to be utterly foreign.
Let my renderings," he continues, " be heard, as Pope
or even Cowper has been heard, and no one will be
' surprised.' "

But the whole question is here. The translator
must not assume that to have taken place which has
not taken place, although, perhaps, he may wish it
to have taken place,—namely, that his diction is
become an established possession of the minds of
men, and therefore is, in its proper place, familiar
to them, will not " surprise " them. If Homer's
language was familiar,—that is, often heard,—then
to this language words like *londis* and *libbard*, which
are not familiar, offer, for the translator's purpose,
no parallel. For some purpose of the philologer
they may offer a parallel to it; for the translator's
purpose they offer none. The question is not,
whether a diction is antiquated for current speech,
but whether it is antiquated for that particular purpose for which it is employed. A diction that is
antiquated for common speech and common prose,
may very well not be antiquated for poetry or certain
special kinds of prose. " Peradventure there shall
be ten found there," is not antiquated for Biblical
prose, though for conversation or for a newspaper
it is antiquated. " The trumpet spake not to the
arméd throng," is not antiquated for poetry, although
we should not write in a letter, " he *spake* to me," or
say, " the British soldier is *arméd* with the Enfield
rifle." But when language is antiquated for that
particular purpose for which it is employed,—as

numbers of Chaucer's words, for instance, are antiquated for poetry,—such language is a bad representative of language which, like Homer's, was never
antiquated for that particular purpose for which it
was employed. I imagine that Πηληϊάδεω for Πηλεί-
δου, in Homer, no more sounded antiquated to
Sophocles than *arméd* for *arm'd*, in Milton, sounds
antiquated to us; but Mr. Newman's *withouten* and
muchel do sound to us antiquated, even for poetry,
and therefore they do not correspond in their effect
upon us with Homer's words in their effect
upon Sophocles. When Chaucer, who uses such
words, is to pass current amongst us, to be familiar
to us, as Homer was familiar to the Athenians, he
has to be modernised, as Wordsworth and others set
to work to modernise him; but an Athenian no more
needed to have Homer modernised, than we need to
have the Bible modernised, or Wordsworth himself.

Therefore, when Mr. Newman's words *bragly*,
bulkin, and the rest, are an established possession
of our minds, as Homer's words were an established
possession of an Athenian's mind, he may use them;
but not till then. Chaucer's words, the words of
Burns, great poets as these were, are yet not thus
an established possession of an Englishman's mind,
and therefore they must not be used in rendering
Homer into English.

Mr. Newman has been misled just by doing that
which his admirer praises him for doing, by taking a
"far broader historical and philological view than"
mine. Precisely because he has done this, and has

applied the "philological view" where it was not applicable, but where the "poetical view" alone was rightly applicable, he has fallen into error.

It is the same with him in his remarks on the difficulty and obscurity of Homer. Homer, I say, is perfectly plain in speech, simple, and intelligible. And I infer from this that his translator, too, ought to be perfectly plain in speech, simple, and intelligible; ought not to say, for instance, in rendering

Οὔτε κε σὲ στέλλοιμι μάχην ἐς κυδιάνειραν . . .

"Nor liefly thee would I advance to man-ennobling battle,"—and things of that kind. Mr. Newman hands me a list of some twenty hard words, invokes Buttman, Mr. Malden, and M. Benfey, and asks me if I think myself wiser than all the world of Greek scholars, and if I am ready to supply the deficiencies of Liddell and Scott's *Lexicon*! But here, again, Mr. Newman errs by not perceiving that the question is one not of scholarship, but of a poetical translation of Homer. This, I say, should be perfectly simple and intelligible. He replies by telling me that ἀδινὸς, εἰλίποδες, and σιγαλόεις are hard words. Well, but what does he infer from that? That the poetical translation, in his rendering of them, is to give us a sense of the difficulties of the scholar, and so is to make his translation obscure? If he does not mean that, how, by bringing forward these hard words, does he touch the question whether an English version of Homer should be plain or not plain? If Homer's poetry, as poetry, is in its general effect on the poetical reader perfectly simple and intelligible, the uncertainty of the scholar about the true meaning of certain words can never change this general effect. Rather will the poetry of Homer make us forget his philology, than his philology make us forget his poetry. It may even be affirmed that every one who reads Homer perpetually for the sake of enjoying his poetry (and no one who does not so read him will ever translate him well), comes at last to form a perfectly clear sense in his own mind for every important word in Homer, such as ἀδινὸς, or ἠλίβατος, whatever the scholar's doubts about the word may be. And this sense is present to his mind with perfect clearness and fulness, whenever the word recurs, although as a scholar he may know that he cannot be sure whether this sense is the right one or not. But poetically he feels clearly about the word, although philologically he may not. The scholar in him may hesitate, like the father in Sheridan's play; but the reader of poetry in him is, like the governor, fixed. The same thing happens to us with our own language. How many words occur in the Bible, for instance, to which thousands of hearers do not feel sure they attach the precise real meaning; but they make out *a* meaning for them out of what materials they have at hand; and the words, heard over and over again, come to convey this meaning with a certainty which poetically is adequate, though not philologically. How many have attached a clear and poetically adequate sense to "the *beam*" and "the *mote*," though not precisely the right one! How clearly, again, have readers got a sense from Milton's words, "grate on their *scrannel* pipes," who yet might have been puzzled to write a commentary on the word *scrannel* for the dictionary! So we get a clear sense from ἀδινὸς as an epithet for grief, after often meeting with it and finding out all we can about it, even though that all be philologically insufficient; so we get a clear sense from εἰλίποδες as an epithet for cows. And this his clear poetical sense about the words, not his philological uncertainties about them, is what the translator has to convey. Words like *bragly* and *bulkin* offer no parallel to these words; because the reader, from his entire want of familiarity with the words *bragly* and *bulkin*, has no clear sense of them poetically.

Perplexed by his knowledge of the philological aspect of Homer's language, encumbered by his own learning, Mr. Newman, I say, misses the poetical aspect, misses that with which alone we are here concerned. "Homer *is* odd," he persists, fixing his eyes on his own philological analysis of ͱώνυξ, and μέροψs, and Κυλλοποδίων, and not on these words in their synthetic character;—just as Professor Max Müller, going a little farther back, and fixing his attention on the elementary value of the word θυγάτηρ, might say Homer was "odd" for using *that* word;—"if the whole Greek nation, by long familiarity, had become inobservant of Homer's oddities,"—of the oddities of this "noble barbarian," as Mr. Newman elsewhere calls him, this "noble barbarian" with the "lively

eye of the savage,"—"that would be no fault of mine.
That would not justify Mr. Arnold's blame of me for
rendering the words correctly." *Correctly,*—ah, but
what *is* correctness in this case? This correctness of
his is the very rock on which Mr. Newman has split.
He is so correct that at last he finds peculiarity
everywhere. The true knowledge of Homer becomes
at last, in his eyes, a knowledge of Homer's "peculiarities, pleasant and unpleasant." Learned men
know these "peculiarities," and Homer is to be translated because the unlearned are impatient to know
them too. "That," he exclaims, "is just why people
want to read an English Homer,—*to know all his
oddities, just as learned men do.*" Here I am obliged to
shake my head, and to declare that, in spite of all my
respect for Mr. Newman, I cannot go these lengths
with him. He talks of my "monomaniac fancy that
there is nothing quaint or antique in Homer." Terrible learning,—I cannot help in my turn exclaim-
ing,—terrible learning, which discovers so much!

Here, then, I take my leave of Mr. Newman,
retaining my opinion that his version of Homer is
spoiled by his making Homer odd and ignoble; but
having, I hope, sufficient love for literature to be able
to canvass works without thinking of persons, and to
hold this or that production cheap, while retaining a
sincere respect, on other grounds, for its author.

In fulfilment of my promise to take this opportunity for giving the translator of Homer a little
further advice, I proceed to notice one or two other
criticisms which I find, in like manner, *suggestive;*

which give us an opportunity, that is, of seeing more
clearly, as we look into them, the true principles on
which translation of Homer should rest. This is all I
seek in criticisms; and, perhaps (as I have already
said) it is only as one seeks a positive result of this
kind, that one can get any fruit from them. Seeking
a negative result from them,—personal altercation and
wrangling,—one gets no fruit; seeking a positive
result,—the elucidation and establishment of one's
ideas,—one may get much. Even bad criticisms may
thus be made suggestive and fruitful. I declared, in
a former lecture on this subject, my conviction that
criticism is not the strong point of our national
literature. Well, even the bad criticisms on our
present topic which I meet with, serve to illustrate
this conviction for me. And thus one is enabled,
even in reading remarks which for Homeric criticism,
for their immediate subject, have no value,—which
are far too personal in spirit, far too immoderate in
temper, and far too heavy-handed in style, for the
delicate matter they have to treat,—still to gain light
and confirmation for a serious idea, and to follow the
Baconian injunction, *semper aliquid addiscere*, always to
be adding to one's stock of observation and knowledge.
Yes, even when we have to do with writers who,—to
quote the words of an exquisite critic, the master of
us all in criticism, M. Sainte-Beuve,—remind us, when
they handle such subjects as our present, of " Romans
of the fourth or fifth century, coming to hold forth,
all at random, in African style, on papers found in
the desk of Augustus, Mæcenas, or Pollio,"—even

then we may instruct ourselves if we may regard ideas and not persons; even then we may enable ourselves to say, with the same critic describing the effect made upon him by D'Argenson's *Memoirs:* " My taste is revolted, but I learn something ;—*Je suis choqué mais je suis instruit.*"

But let us pass to criticisms which are suggestive directly and not thus indirectly only,—criticisms by examining which we may be brought nearer to what immediately interests us,—the right way of translating Homer.

I said that Homer did not rise and sink with his subject, was never to be called prosaic and low. This gives surprise to many persons, who object that parts of the *Iliad* are certainly pitched lower than others, and who remind me of a number of absolutely level passages in Homer. But I never denied that a *subject* must rise and sink, that it must have its elevated and its level regions; all I deny is, that a poet can be said to rise and sink when all that he, as a poet, can do, is perfectly well done; when he is perfectly sound and good, that is, perfect as a poet, in the level regions of his subject as well as in its elevated regions. Indeed, what distinguishes the greatest masters of poetry from all others is, that they are perfectly sound and poetical in these level regions of their subject,—in these regions which are the great difficulty of all poets but the very greatest, which they never quite know what to do with. A poet may sink in these regions by being falsely grand as well as by being low; he sinks, in short, whenever he does not treat his matter, whatever it is, in a perfectly good and poetic way. But, so long as he treats it in this way, he cannot be said to *sink*, whatever his matter may do. A passage of the simplest narrative is quoted to me from Homer :—

ὤτρυνεν δὲ ἕκαστον ἐποιχόμενος ἐπέεσσιν,
Μέσθλην τε, Γλαῦκόν τε, Μέδοντά τε, Θερσίλοχόν τε . . .[1]

and I am asked, whether Homer does not sink *there ;* whether he " *can* have intended such lines as those for poetry ? " My answer is : Those lines are very good poetry indeed, poetry of the best class, *in that place.* But when Wordsworth, having to narrate a very plain matter, tries *not* to sink in narrating it, tries, in short, to be what is falsely called poetical, he does sink, although he sinks by being pompous, not by being low.

> " Onward we drove beneath the Castle ; caught,
> While crossing Magdalen Bridge, a glimpse of Cam,
> And at the Hoop alighted, famous inn."

That last line shows excellently how a poet may sink with his subject by resolving not to sink with it. A page or two farther on, the subject rises to grandeur, and then Wordsworth is nobly worthy of it :—

> " The antechapel, where the statue stood
> Of Newton with his prism and silent face,
> The marble index of a mind for ever
> Voyaging through strange seas of thought, alone."

But the supreme poet is he who is thoroughly sound and poetical, alike when his subject is grand, and when it is plain : with him the subject may sink, but

[1] *Iliad*, xvii. 216.

never the poet. But a Dutch painter does not rise
and sink with his subject,—Defoe, in *Moll Flanders*,
does not rise and sink with his subject,—in so far as
an artist cannot be said to sink who is sound in his
treatment of his subject, however plain it is : yet
Defoe, yet a Dutch painter, may in one sense be said
to sink with their subject, because though sound in
their treatment of it, they are not *poetical*,—poetical
in the true, not the false sense of the word ; because,
in fact, they are not in the grand style. Homer can
in no sense be said to sink with his subject, because
his soundness has something more than literal naturalness about it ; because his soundness is the soundness
of Homer, of a great epic poet ; because, in fact, he is
in the grand style. So he sheds over the simplest
matter he touches the charm of his grand manner ;
he makes everything noble. Nothing has raised more
questioning among my critics than these words,—
noble, the grand style. People complain that I do not
define these words sufficiently, that I do not tell them
enough about them. "The grand style,—but what
is the grand style ?"—they cry ; some with an incli-
nation to believe in it, but puzzled ; others mockingly
and with incredulity. Alas ! the grand style is the
last matter in the world for verbal definition to deal
with adequately. One may say of it as is said of
faith : "One must feel it in order to know what it
is." But, as of faith, so too one may say of nobleness, of the grand style : "Woe to those who know
it not !" Yet this expression, though indefinable, has
a charm ; one is the better for considering it ; *bonum*

est, nos hic esse; nay, one loves to try to explain it, though one knows that one must speak imperfectly. For those, then, who ask the question,—What is the grand style?—with sincerity, I will try to make some answer, inadequate as it must be. For those who ask it mockingly I have no answer, except to repeat to them, with compassionate sorrow, the Gospel words: *Moriemini in peccatis vestris,*—Ye shall die in your sins.

But let me, at any rate, have the pleasure of again giving, before I begin to try and define the grand style, a specimen of what it *is.*

> " Standing on earth, not rapt above the pole,
> More safe I sing with mortal voice, unchanged
> To hoarse or mute, though fall'n on evil days,
> On evil days though fall'n, and evil tongues." . . .

There is the grand style in perfection; and any one who has a sense for it, will feel it a thousand times better from repeating those lines than from hearing anything I can say about it.

Let us try, however, what *can* be said, controlling what we say by examples. I think it will be found that the grand style arises in poetry, *when a noble nature, poetically gifted, treats with simplicity or with severity a serious subject.* I think this definition will be found to cover all instances of the grand style in poetry which present themselves. I think it will be found to exclude all poetry which is not in the grand style. And I think it contains no terms which are obscure, which themselves need defining. Even those who do not understand what is meant by calling poetry noble, will understand, I imagine, what is meant by speaking of a noble nature in a man. But the noble or powerful nature—the *bedeutendes indi-viduum* of Goethe—is not enough. For instance, Mr. Newman has zeal for learning, zeal for thinking, zeal for liberty, and all these things are noble, they ennoble a man; but he has not the poetical gift: there must be the poetical gift, the "divine faculty," also. And, besides all this, the subject must be a serious one (for it is only by a kind of license that we can speak of the grand style in comedy); and it must be treated *with simplicity or severity.* Here is the great difficulty: the poets of the world have been many; there has been wanting neither abundance of poetical gift nor abundance of noble natures; but a poetical gift so happy, in a noble nature so circumstanced and trained, that the result is a continuous style, perfect in simplicity or perfect in severity, has been extremely rare. One poet has had the gifts of nature and faculty in unequalled fulness, without the circumstances and training which make this sustained perfection of style possible. Of other poets, some have caught this perfect strain now and then, in short pieces or single lines, but have not been able to maintain it through considerable works; others have composed all their productions in a style which, by comparison with the best, one must call secondary.

The best model of the grand style simple is Homer; perhaps the best model of the grand style severe is Milton. But Dante is remarkable for affording admirable examples of both styles; he has the grand style which arises from simplicity, and he has the grand style which arises from severity; and from him I will illustrate them both. In a former lecture I pointed out what that severity of poetical style is, which comes from saying a thing with a kind of intense compression, or in an allusive, brief, almost haughty way, as if the poet's mind were charged with so many and such grave matters, that he would not deign to treat any one of them explicitly. Of this severity the last line of the following stanza of the *Purgatory* is a good example. Dante has been telling Forese that Virgil had guided him through Hell, and he goes on :—

> "Indi m' han tratto su gli suoi conforti,
> Salendo e rigirando la Montagna
> *Che drizza voi che il mondo fece torti.*"[1]

"Thence hath his comforting aid led me up, climbing and circling the Mountain, *which straightens you whom the world made crooked.*" These last words, "la Montagna *che drizza voi che il mondo fece torti.*"—"the Mountain *which straightens you whom the world made crooked,*"—for the Mountain of Purgatory, I call an excellent specimen of the grand style in severity, where the poet's mind is too full charged to suffer him to speak more explicitly. But the very next stanza is a beautiful specimen of the grand style in simplicity, where a noble nature and a poetical gift unite to utter a thing with the most limpid plainness and clearness :—

> "Tanto dice di farmi sua compagna
> Ch' io sarò là dove fia Beatrice;
> Quivi convien che senza lui rimagna."[2]

---

[1] *Purgatory*, xxiii. 124.   [2] *Ibid.* xxiii. 127.

"So long," Dante continues, "so long he (Virgil) saith he will bear me company, until I shall be there where Beatrice is; there it behoves that without him I remain." But the noble simplicity of that in the Italian no words of mine can render.

Both these styles, the simple and the severe, are truly grand; the severe seems, perhaps, the grandest, so long as we attend most to the great personality, to the noble nature, in the poet its author; the simple seems the grandest when we attend most to the exquisite faculty, to the poetical gift. But the simple is no doubt to be preferred. It is the more *magical:* in the other there is something intellectual, something which gives scope for a play of thought which may exist where the poetical gift is either wanting or present in only inferior degree: the severe is much more imitable, and this a little spoils its charm. A kind of semblance of this style keeps Young going, one may say, through all the nine parts of that most indifferent production, the *Night Thoughts.* But the grand style in simplicity is inimitable:

αἰὼν ἀσφαλὴς

οὐκ ἔγεντ' οὔτ' Αἰακίδᾳ παρὰ Πηλεῖ,

οὔτε παρ' ἀντιθέῳ Κάδμῳ · λέγονται μὰν βροτῶν

ὄλβον ὑπέρτατον οἳ σχεῖν, οἵ τε καὶ χρυσαμπύκων

μελπομενᾶν ἐν ὄρει Μοισᾶν, καὶ ἐν ἑπταπύλοις

ἄϊον Θήβαις . . .[1]

---

[1] "A secure time fell to the lot neither of Peleus the son of Æacus, nor of the godlike Cadmus; howbeit these are said to have had, of all mortals, the supreme of happiness, who heard the golden-snooded Muses sing, one of them on the mountain (Pelion), the other in seven-gated Thebes."

There is a limpidness in that, a want of salient points to seize and transfer, which makes imitation impossible, except by a genius akin to the genius which produced it.

Greek simplicity and Greek grace are inimitable; but it is said that the *Iliad* may still be ballad-poetry while infinitely superior to all other ballads, and that, in my specimens of English ballad-poetry, I have been unfair. Well, no doubt there are better things in English ballad-poetry than

" Now Christ thee save, thou proud portér," . . .

but the real strength of a chain, they say, is the strength of its weakest link; and what I was trying to show you was, that the English ballad-style is not an instrument of enough compass and force to correspond to the Greek hexameter; that, owing to an inherent weakness in it as an epic style, it easily runs into one of two faults,—either it is prosaic and humdrum, or, trying to avoid that fault, and to make itself lively (*se faire vif*), it becomes pert and jaunty. To show that, the passage about King Adland's porter serves very well. But these degradations are not proper to a true epic instrument, such as the Greek hexameter.

You may say, if you like, when you find Homer's verse, even in describing the plainest matter, neither humdrum nor jaunty, that this is because he is so incomparably better a poet than other balladists, because he is Homer. But take the whole range of Greek epic poetry,—take the later poets, the poets of

the last ages of this poetry, many of them most
indifferent, — Coluthus, Tryphiodorus, Quintus of
Smyrna, Nonnus. Never will you find in this instrument of the hexameter, even in their hands, the
vices of the ballad-style in the weak moments of this
last: everywhere the hexameter—a noble, a truly
epical instrument—rather resists the weakness of its
employer than lends itself to it. Quintus of Smyrna
is a poet of merit, but certainly not a poet of a high
order; with him, too, epic poetry, whether in the
character of its prosody or in that of its diction, is no
longer the epic poetry of earlier and better times, nor
epic poetry as again restored by Nonnus: but even in
Quintus of Smyrna, I say, the hexameter is still the
hexameter; it is a style which the ballad-style, even
in the hands of better poets, cannot rival. And in
the hands of inferior poets, the ballad-style sinks to
vices of which the hexameter, even in the hands of a
Tryphiodorus, never can become guilty.

But a critic, whom it is impossible to read without
pleasure, and the disguise of whose initials I am sure
I may be allowed to penetrate,—Mr. Spedding,—says
that he "denies altogether that the metrical movement of the English hexameter has any resemblance
to that of the Greek." Of course, in that case, if the
two metres in no respect correspond, praise accorded
to the Greek hexameter as an epical instrument will
not extend to the English. Mr. Spedding seeks to
establish his proposition by pointing out that the
system of accentuation differs in the English and in
the Virgilian hexameter; that in the first, the accent

and the long syllable (or what has to do duty as such) coincide, in the second they do not. He says that we cannot be so sure of the accent with which Greek verse should be read as of that with which Latin should; but that the lines of Homer in which the accent and the long syllable coincide, as in the English hexameter, are certainly very rare. He suggests a type of English hexameter in agreement with the Virgilian model, and formed on the supposition that "quantity is as distinguishable in English as in Latin or Greek by any ear that will attend to it." Of the truth of this supposition he entertains no doubt. The new hexameter will, Mr. Spedding thinks, at least have the merit of resembling, in its metrical movement, the classical hexameter, which merit the ordinary English hexameter has not. But even with this improved hexameter he is not satisfied; and he goes on, first to suggest other metres for rendering Homer, and finally to suggest that rendering Homer is impossible.

A scholar to whom all who admire Lucretius owe a large debt of gratitude,—Mr. Munro,—has replied to Mr. Spedding. Mr. Munro declares that "the accent of the old Greeks and Romans resembled our accent only in name, in reality was essentially different;" that "our English reading of Homer and Virgil has in itself no meaning;" and that "accent has nothing to do with the Virgilian hexameter." If this be so, of course the merit which Mr. Spedding attributes to his own hexameter, of really corresponding with the Virgilian hexameter, has no existence.

Again ; in contradiction to Mr. Spedding's assertion that lines in which (in our reading of them) the accent and the long syllable coincide,[1] as in the ordinary English hexameter, are "rare even in Homer," Mr. Munro declares that such lines, "instead of being rare, are among the very commonest types of Homeric rhythm." Mr. Spedding asserts that " quantity is as distinguishable in English as in Latin or Greek by any ear that will attend to it ; " but Mr. Munro replies, that in English " neither his ear nor his reason recognises any real distinction of quantity except that which is produced by accentuated and unaccentuated syllables." He therefore arrives at the conclusion that in constructing English hexa-meters, " quantity must be utterly discarded ; and longer or shorter unaccentuated syllables can have no meaning, except so far as they may be made to pro-duce sweeter or harsher sounds in the hands of a master."

It is not for me to interpose between two such combatants ; and indeed my way lies, not up the highroad where they are contending, but along a bypath. With the absolute truth of their general propositions respecting accent and quantity, I have nothing to do ; it is most interesting and instructive to me to hear such propositions discussed, when it is Mr. Munro or Mr. Spedding who discusses them ; but I have strictly limited myself in these Lectures to the humble function of giving practical advice to

---

[1] Lines such as the first of the *Odyssey* :

Ἄνδρα μοι ἔννεπε, Μοῦσα, πολύτροπον, ὃς μάλα πολλα . . .

the translator of Homer. He, I still think, must not follow so confidently, as makers of English hexameters have hitherto followed, Mr. Munro's maxim,—*quantity may be utterly discarded*. He must not, like Mr. Longfellow, make *seventeen* a dactyl in spite of all the length of its last syllable, even though he can plead that in counting we lay the accent on the first syllable of this word. He may be far from attaining Mr. Spedding's nicety of ear;—may be unable to feel that " while *quantity* is a dactyl, *quiddity* is a tribrach," and that "*rapidly* is a word to which we find no parallel in Latin;"—but I think he must bring himself to distinguish, with Mr. Spedding, between "*th' o'er-*wearied eyelid," and "*the* wearied eyelid," as being, the one a correct ending for a hexameter, the other an ending with a false quantity in it; instead of finding, with Mr. Munro, that this distinction "conveys to his mind no intelligible idea." He must temper his belief in Mr. Munro's dictum,—*quantity must be utterly discarded*,—by mixing with it a belief in this other dictum of the same author,—*two or more consonants take longer time in enunciating than one.*[1]

[1] Substantially, however, in the question at issue between Mr. Munro and Mr. Spedding, I agree with Mr. Munro. By the italicised words in the following sentence, "The rhythm of the Virgilian hexameter depends entirely on *cœsura, pause*, and a due arrangement of words," he has touched, it seems to me, in the constitution of this hexameter, the central point, which Mr. Spedding misses. The accent, or *heightened tone*, of Virgil in reading his own hexameters, was probably far from being the same thing as the accent or *stress* with which we read them. The general effect of each line, in Virgil's mouth, was probably therefore something widely different from what Mr. Spedding

Criticism is so apt in general to be vague and impalpable, that when it gives us a solid and definite possession, such as is Mr. Spedding's parallel of the Virgilian and the English hexameter with their difference of accentuation distinctly marked, we cannot be too grateful to it. It is in the way in which Mr. Spedding proceeds to press his conclusions from the parallel which he has drawn out, that his criticism seems to me to come a little short. Here even he, I think, shows (if he will allow me to say so) a little of that want of pliancy and suppleness so common among critics, but so dangerous to their criticism ; he is a little too absolute in imposing his metrical laws ; he too much forgets the excellent maxim of Menander, so applicable to literary criticism :—

> Καλὸν οἱ νόμοι σφόδρ' εἰσίν· ὁ δ' ὁρῶν τοὺς νόμους
> λίαν ἀκριβῶς, συκοφάντης φαίνεται·

"Laws are admirable things ; but he who keeps his eye too closely fixed upon them, runs the risk of becoming "—let us say, a purist.   Mr. Spedding is

assumes it to have been : an ancient's accentual reading was something which allowed the metrical beat of the Latin line to be far more perceptible than our accentual reading allows it to be.

On the question as to the *real* rhythm of the ancient hexameter, Mr. Newman has in his *Reply* a page quite admirable for force and precision.   Here he is in his element, and his ability and acuteness have their proper scope.   But it is true that the *modern* reading of the ancient hexameter is what the modern hexameter has to imitate, and that the English reading of the Virgilian hexameter is as Mr. Spedding describes it. Why this reading has not been imitated by the English hexameter, I have tried to point out in the text.

probably mistaken in supposing that Virgil pronounced his hexameters as Mr. Spedding pronounces them. He is almost certainly mistaken in supposing that Homer pronounced his hexameters as Mr. Spedding pronounces Virgil's. But this, as I have said, is not a question for us to treat; all we are here concerned with is the imitation, by the English hexameter, of the ancient hexameter *in its effect upon us moderns.* Suppose we concede to Mr. Spedding that his parallel proves our accentuation of the English and of the Virgilian hexameter to be different: what are we to conclude from that; how will a criticism—not a formal, but a substantial criticism—deal with such a fact as that? Will it infer, as Mr. Spedding infers, that the English hexameter, therefore, must not pretend to reproduce better than other rhythms the movement of Homer's hexameter for us,—that there can be no correspondence at all between the movement of these two hexameters,—that if we want to have such a correspondence, we must abandon the current English hexameter altogether, and adopt in its place a new hexameter of Mr. Spedding's Anglo-Latin type,— substitute for lines like the

" Clearly the rest I behold of the dark-eyed sons of Achaia " . .

of Dr. Hawtrey, lines like the

" Procession, complex melodies, pause, quantity, accent,
    After Virgilian precedent and practice, in order " . . .

of Mr. Spedding? To infer this, is to go, as I have complained of Mr. Newman for sometimes going, a great deal too fast. I think prudent criticism must certainly recognise, in the current English hexameter, a fact which cannot so lightly be set aside; it must acknowledge that by this hexameter the English ear, the genius of the English language, have, in their own way, adopted, have *translated* for themselves the Homeric hexameter; and that a rhythm which has thus grown up, which is thus, in a manner, the production of nature, has in its general type something necessary and inevitable, something which admits change only within narrow limits, which precludes change that is sweeping and essential. I think, therefore, the prudent critic will regard Mr. Spedding's proposed revolution as simply impracticable. He will feel that in English poetry the hexameter, if used at all, must be, in the main, the English hexameter now current. He will perceive that its having come into existence as the representative of the Homeric hexameter, proves it to have, for the English ear, a certain correspondence with the Homeric hexameter, although this correspondence may be, from the difference of the Greek and English languages, necessarily incomplete. This incompleteness he will endeavour,[1] as he may find or fancy himself able,

---

[1] Such a minor change I have attempted by occasionally shifting, in the first foot of the hexameter, the accent from the first syllable to the second. In the current English hexameter, it is on the first. Mr. Spedding, who proposes radically to subvert the constitution of this hexameter, seems not to understand that any one can propose to modify it partially; he can comprehend revolution in this metre, but not reform. Accordingly he asks me how I can bring myself to say, "*Bét*ween that and the ships," or "*Thére* sat fifty men;" or how I can reconcile such forcing of the accent with my own rule, that

gradually somewhat to lessen through minor changes, suggested by the ancient hexameter, but respecting the general constitution of the modern : the notion of making it disappear altogether by the critic's inventing in his closet a new constitution of his own for the English hexameter, he will judge to be a chimerical dream.

When, therefore, Mr. Spedding objects to the English hexameter, that it imperfectly represents the movement of the ancient hexameters, I answer : We

"hexameters must *read themselves.*" Presently he says that he cannot believe I do pronounce these words so, but that he thinks I leave out the accent in the first foot altogether, and thus get a hexameter with only five accents. He will pardon me : I pronounce, as I suppose he himself does, if he reads the words naturally, "Be*tween* that and the ships," and "there *sát* fifty men." Mr. Spedding is familiar enough with this accent on the second syllable in Virgil's hexameters ; in "et *té* montosa," or "Ve*ló*ces jaculo." Such a change is an attempt to relieve the monotony of the current English hexameter by occasionally altering the position of one of its accents ; it is not an attempt to make a wholly new English hexameter by habitually altering the position of four of them. Very likely it is an unsuccessful attempt ; but at any rate it does not violate what I think is the fundamental rule for English hexameters,— that they be such as to *read themselves* without necessitating, on the reader's part, any non-natural putting-on or taking-off accent. Hexameters like these of Mr. Longfellow,

"In that delightful land which is washed by the Delaware's
    waters,"

and,

"As if they fain would appease the Dryads, whose haunts they
    molested,"

violate this rule ; and they are very common. I think the blemish of Mr. Dart's recent meritorious version of the *Iliad* is that it contains too many of them.

must work with the tools we have. The received
English type, in its general outlines, is, for England,
the necessary given type of this metre; it is by
rendering the metrical beat of its pattern, not by
rendering the accentual beat of it, that the English
language has adapted the Greek hexameter.   To
render the metrical beat of its pattern is something;
by effecting so much as this the English hexameter
puts itself in closer relations with its original, it
comes nearer to its movement than any other metre
which does not even effect so much as this; but Mr.
Spedding is dissatisfied with it for not effecting more
still, for not rendering the accentual beat too.   If he
asks me *why* the English hexameter has not tried to
render this too, *why* it has confined itself to rendering
the metrical beat, *why*, in short, it is itself, and not
Mr. Spedding's new hexameter,—that is a question
which I, whose only business is to give practical
advice to a translator, am not bound to answer; but
I will not decline to answer it nevertheless.   I will
suggest to Mr. Spedding that, as I have already said,
the modern hexameter is merely an attempt to imitate
the effect of the ancient hexameter, as read by us
moderns; that the great object of its imitation has
been the hexameter of Homer; that of this hexameter
such lines as those which Mr. Spedding declares to
be so rare, even in Homer, but which are in truth
so common,—lines in which the quantity and the
reader's accent coincide,—are, for the English reader,
just from that simplicity (for him) of rhythm which
they owe to this very coincidence, the master-type;

that so much is this the case, that one may again and
again notice an English reader of Homer, in reading
lines where his Virgilian accent would not coincide
with the quantity, abandoning this accent, and reading the lines (as we say) *by quantity*, reading them as
if he were scanning them; while foreigners neglect
our Virgilian accent even in reading Virgil, read even
Virgil by quantity, making the accents coincide with
the long syllables. And no doubt the hexameter of
a kindred language, the German, based on this mode
of reading the ancient hexameter, has had a powerful
influence upon the type of its English fellow. But
all this shows how extremely powerful accent is for
us moderns, since we find not even Greek and Latin
quantity perceptible enough without it. Yet in these
languages, where we have been accustomed always to
look for it, it is far more perceptible to us Englishmen
than in our own language, where we have not been
accustomed to look for it. And here is the true
reason why Mr. Spedding's hexameter is not and
cannot be the current English hexameter, even though
it is based on the accentuation which Englishmen
give to all Virgil's lines, and to many of Homer's,—
that the quantity which in Greek or Latin words we
feel, or imagine we feel, even though it be unsupported by accent, we do not feel or imagine we feel
in English words when it is thus unsupported. For
example, in repeating the Latin line

"Ipsa tibi blandos *fundent* cunabula flores,

an Englishman feels the length of the second syllable

of *fundent*, although he lays the accent on the first;
but in repeating Mr. Spedding's line,

' Softly cometh slumber *closing* th' o'erwearied eyelid,"

the English ear, full of the accent on the first syllable
of *closing*, has really no sense at all of any length in
its second.   The metrical beat of the line is thus
quite destroyed.

So when Mr. Spedding proposes a new Anglo-
Virgilian hexameter he proposes an impossibility;
when he "denies altogether that the metrical movement of the English hexameter has *any* resemblance
to that of the Greek," he denies too much; when he
declares that, "were every other metre impossible,
an attempt to translate Homer into English hexameters
might be permitted, *but that such an attempt he himself
would never read*," he exhibits, it seems to me, a little
of that obduracy and over-vehemence in liking and
disliking, — a remnant, I suppose, of our insular
ferocity, — to which English criticism is so prone.
He ought to be enchanted to meet with a good
attempt in any metre, even though he would never
have advised it, even though its success be contrary
to all his expectations; for it is the critic's first duty
—prior even to his duty of stigmatising what is bad—
to welcome everything that is good.   In welcoming this,
he must at all times be ready, like the Christian con-
vert, even to burn what he used to worship, and to
worship what he used to burn.   Nay, but he need
not be thus inconsistent in welcoming it; he may
retain all his principles : principles endure, circum-

stances change; absolute success is one thing, relative success another. Relative success may take place under the most diverse conditions; and it is in appreciating the good in even relative success, it is in taking into account the change of circumstances, that the critic's judgment is tested, that his versatility must display itself. He is to keep his idea of the best, of perfection, and at the same time to be willingly accessible to every second best which offers itself. So I enjoy the ease and beauty of Mr. Spedding's stanza,

> "Therewith to all the gods in order due . . ."

I welcome it, in the absence of equally good poetry in another metre,[1] although I still think the stanza

---

[1] As I welcome another more recent attempt in stanza,—Mr. Worsley's version of the *Odyssey* in Spenser's measure. Mr. Worsley does me the honour to notice some remarks of mine on this measure: I had said that its greater intricacy made it a worse measure than even the ten-syllable couplet to employ for rendering Homer. He points out, in answer, that "the more complicated the correspondences in a poetical measure, the less obtrusive and absolute are the rhymes." This is true, and subtly remarked; but I never denied that the single shocks of rhyme in the couplet were more *strongly felt* than those in the stanza; I said that the more frequent recurrence of the same rhyme, in the stanza, necessarily made this measure more *intricate*. The stanza repacks Homer's matter yet more arbitrarily, and therefore changes his movement yet more radically, than the couplet. Accordingly, I imagine a nearer approach to a perfect translation of Homer is possible in the couplet, well managed, than in the stanza, however well managed. But meanwhile Mr. Worsley,—applying the Spenserian stanza, that beautiful romantic measure, to the most romantic poem of the ancient world; making this stanza yield him, too (what it never yielded to Byron), its treasures of fluidity and sweet ease;

unfit to render Homer thoroughly well,—although I still think other metres fit to render him better. So I concede to Mr. Spedding that every form of translation, prose or verse, must more or less break up Homer in order to reproduce him; but then I urge that that form which needs to break him up least is to be preferred. So I concede to him that the test proposed by me for the translator—a competent scholar's judgment whether the translation more or less reproduces for him the effect of the original— is not perfectly satisfactory; but I adopt it as the best we can get, as the only test capable of being really applied; for Mr. Spedding's proposed substitute —the translations making the same effect, more or less, upon the unlearned which the original makes upon the scholar—is a test which can never really be applied at all. These two impressions—that of the scholar, and that of the unlearned reader — can, practically, never be accurately compared; they are, and must remain, like those lines we read of in Euclid, which, though produced ever so far, can never meet. So, again, I concede that a good verse-translation of Homer, or, indeed, of any poet, is very difficult, and that a good prose-translation is much easier; but then I urge that a verse-translation, while giving the pleasure which Pope's has given, might at the same time render Homer more faithfully above all, bringing to his task a truly poetical sense and skill, —has produced a version of the *Odyssey* much the most pleasing of those hitherto produced, and which is delightful to read.

For the public this may well be enough, nay, more than enough; but for the critic even this is not yet quite enough.

than Pope's ; and that this being possible, we ought
not to cease wishing for a source of pleasure which
no prose-translation can ever hope to rival.

Wishing for such a verse-translation of Homer,
believing that rhythms have natural tendencies which,
within certain limits, inevitably govern them ; having
little faith, therefore, that rhythms which have manifested tendencies utterly un-Homeric can so change
themselves as to become well adapted for rendering
Homer,—I have looked about for the rhythm which
seems to depart least from the tendencies of Homer's
rhythm. Such a rhythm I think may be found in
the English hexameter, somewhat modified. I look
with hope towards continued attempts at perfecting
and employing this rhythm ; but my belief in the
immediate success of such attempts is far less con-
fident than has been supposed. Between the recognition of this rhythm as ideally the best, and the
recommendation of it to the translator for instant
practical use, there must come all that consideration
of circumstances, all that pliancy in foregoing, under
the pressure of certain difficulties, the absolute best,
which I have said is so indispensable to the critic.
The hexameter is, comparatively, still unfamiliar in
England ; many people have a great dislike to it. A
certain degree of unfamiliarity, a certain degree of dislike, are obstacles with which it is not wise to contend.
It is difficult to say at present whether the dislike to
this rhythm is so strong and so wide-spread that it
will prevent its ever becoming thoroughly familiar.
I think not, but it is too soon to decide. I am in-

clined to think that the dislike of it is rather among the professional critics than among the general public; I think the reception which Mr. Longfellow's *Evangeline* has met with indicates this. I think that even now, if a version of the *Iliad* in English hexameters were made by a poet who, like Mr. Longfellow, has that indefinable quality which renders him popular,— something *attractive* in his talent, which communicates itself to his verses,—it would have a great success among the general public. Yet a version of Homer in hexameters of the *Evangeline* type would not satisfy the judicious, nor is the definite establishment of this type to be desired ; and one would regret that Mr. Longfellow should, even to popularise the hexameter, give the immense labour required for a translation of Homer, when one could not wish his work to stand. Rather it is to be wished that by the efforts of poets like Mr. Longfellow in original poetry, and the efforts of less distinguished poets in the task of translation, the hexameter may gradually be made familiar to the ear of the English public ; at the same time that there gradually arises, out of all these efforts, an improved type of this rhythm ; a type which some man of genius may sign with the final stamp, and employ in rendering Homer ; a hexameter which may be as superior to Vosse's as Shakspeare's blank verse is superior to Schiller's. I am inclined to believe that all this travail will actually take place, because I believe that modern poetry is actually in want of such an instrument as the hexameter.

In the meantime, whether this rhythm be destined to success or not, let us steadily keep in mind what originally made us turn to it. We turned to it because we required certain Homeric characteristics in a translation of Homer, and because all other rhythms seemed to find, from different causes, great difficulties in satisfying this our requirement. If the hexameter is impossible, if one of these other rhythms must be used, let us keep this rhythm always in mind of our requirements and of its own faults, let us compel it to get rid of these latter as much as possible. It may be necessary to have recourse to blank verse; but then blank verse must *de-Cowperise* itself, must get rid of the habits of stiff self-retardation which make it say "*Not fewer* shone," for "*So many shone.*" Homer moves swiftly : blank verse *can* move swiftly if it likes, but it must remember that the movement of such lines as

"A thousand fires were burning, and by each . . ."

is just the slow movement which makes us despair of it. Homer moves with noble ease : blank verse must not be suffered to forget that the movement of

"Came they not over from sweet Lacedæmon . . ."

is ungainly. Homer's expression of his thought is simple as light : we know how blank verse affects such locutions as

"While the steeds *mouthed their corn aloof* . . ."

and such modes of expressing one's thought are sophisticated and artificial.

One sees how needful it is to direct incessantly the English translator's attention to the essential charac-

teristics of Homer's poetry, when so accomplished a
person as Mr. Spedding, recognising these characteristics as indeed Homer's, admitting them to be essential,
is led by the ingrained habits and tendencies of
English blank verse thus repeatedly to lose sight of
them in translating even a few lines.   One sees this
yet more clearly, when Mr. Spedding, taking me to
task for saying that the blank verse used for rendering Homer "must not be Mr. Tennyson's blank
verse," declares that in most of Mr. Tennyson's blank
verse all Homer's essential characteristics—"rapidity
of movement, *plainness of words and style, simplicity and
directness of ideas*, and, above all, nobleness of manner
—are as conspicuous as in Homer himself."   This
shows, it seems to me, how hard it is for English
readers of poetry, even the most accomplished, to feel
deeply and permanently what Greek plainness of
thought and Greek simplicity of expression really
are : they admit the importance of these qualities in
a general way, but they have no ever-present sense of
them ; and they easily attribute them to any poetry
which has other excellent qualities, and which they
very much admire.   No doubt there are plainer
things in Mr. Tennyson's poetry than the three lines
I quoted ; in choosing them, as in choosing a specimen of ballad-poetry, I wished to bring out clearly,
by a strong instance, the qualities of thought and
style to which I was calling attention ; but when Mr.
Spedding talks of a plainness of thought *like Homer's*,
of a plainness of speech *like Homer's*, and says that
he finds these constantly in Mr. Tennyson's poetry, I

answer that these I do not find there at all. Mr.
Tennyson is a most distinguished and charming poet;
but the very essential characteristic of his poetry is,
it seems to me, an extreme subtlety and curious
elaborateness of thought, an extreme subtlety and curious elaborateness of expression. In the best and most
characteristic productions of his genius, these characteristics are most prominent. They are marked characteristics, as we have seen, of the Elizabethan poets;
they are marked, though not the essential, characteristics of Shakspeare himself. Under the influences
of the nineteenth century, under wholly new conditions of thought and culture, they manifest themselves in Mr. Tennyson's poetry in a wholly new way.
But they are still there. The essential bent of his
poetry is towards such expressions as—

> " Now lies the Earth all Danaë to the stars;"

>   "O'er the sun's bright eye
> Drew the vast eyelid of an inky cloud;"

> " When the cairned mountain was a shadow, sunned
> The world to peace again ;"

> " The fresh young captains flashed their glittering teeth,
> The huge bush-bearded barons heaved and blew;"

> " He bared the knotted column of his throat,
> The massive square of his heroic breast,
> And arms on which the standing muscle sloped
> As slopes a wild brook o'er a little stone,
> Running too vehemently to break upon it."

And this way of speaking is the least *plain*, the most
un-Homeric, which can possibly be conceived. Homer
presents his thought to you just as it wells from the
source of his mind : Mr. Tennyson carefully distils his

thought before he will part with it.   Hence comes, in
the expression of the thought, a heightened and elaborate air.   In Homer's poetry it is all natural thoughts
in natural words ; in Mr. Tennyson's poetry it is all
distilled thoughts in distilled words.   Exactly this
heightening and elaboration may be observed in Mr.
Spedding's

> " While the steeds *mouthed their corn aloof*,"

(an expression which might have been Mr. Tennyson's)
on which I have already commented ; and to one who
is penetrated with a sense of the real simplicity of
Homer, this subtle sophistication of the thought is, I
think, very perceptible even in such lines as these,—

> " And drunk delight of battle with my peers,
> Far on the ringing plains of windy Troy,"—

which I have seen quoted as perfectly Homeric.   Perfect simplicity can be obtained only by a genius of
which perfect simplicity is an essential characteristic.

So true is this, that when a genius essentially
subtle, or a genius which, from whatever cause, is in
its essence not truly and broadly simple, determines
to be perfectly plain, determines not to admit a shade
of subtlety or curiosity into its expression, it cannot
ever then attain real simplicity ; it can only attain a
semblance of simplicity.[1]   French criticism, richer in
its vocabulary than ours, has invented a useful word

---

[1] I speak of poetic genius as employing itself upon narrative
or dramatic poetry,—poetry in which the poet has to go out of
himself and to create.   In lyrical poetry, in the direct expression of personal feeling, the most subtle genius may, under the
momentary pressure of passion, express itself simply.   Even
here, however, the native tendency will generally be discernible.

to distinguish this semblance (often very beautiful and valuable) from the real quality. The real quality it calls *simplicité*, the semblance *simplesse*. The one is natural simplicity, the other is artificial simplicity. What is called simplicity in the productions of a genius essentially not simple, is, in truth, *simplesse*. The two are distinguishable from one another the moment they appear in company. For instance, let us take the opening of the narrative in Wordsworth's *Michael :—*

> " Upon the forest-side in Grasmere Vale
> There dwelt a shepherd, Michael was his name ;
> An old man, stout of heart, and strong of limb.
> His bodily frame had been from youth to age
> Of an unusual strength ; his mind was keen,
> Intense, and frugal, apt for all affairs ;
> And in his shepherd's calling he was prompt
> And watchful more than ordinary men."

Now let us take the opening of the narrative in Mr. Tennyson's *Dora :—*

> " With Farmer Allan at the farm abode
> William and Dora. William was his son,
> And she his niece. He often looked at them,
> And often thought, 'I'll make them man and wife.' "

The simplicity of the first of these passages is *simplicité ;* that of the second, *simplesse*. Let us take the end of the same two poems : first, of *Michael :—*

> " The cottage which was named the Evening Star
> Is gone,—the ploughshare has been through the ground
> On which it stood ; great changes have been wrought
> In all the neighbourhood : yet the oak is left
> That grew beside their door : and the remains
> Of the unfinished sheepfold may be seen
> Beside the boisterous brook of Green-head Ghyll."

And now, of *Dora :*—

> " So those four abode
> Within one house together ; and as years
> Went forward, Mary took another mate :
> But Dora lived unmarried till her death."

A heedless critic may call both of these passages simple if he will. Simple, in a certain sense, they both are ; but between the simplicity of the two there is all the difference that there is between the simplicity of Homer and the simplicity of Moschus.

But—whether the hexameter establish itself or not, whether a truly simple and rapid blank verse be obtained or not, as the vehicle for a standard English translation of Homer—I feel sure that this vehicle will not be furnished by the ballad-form. On this question about the ballad-character of Homer's poetry, I see that Professor Blackie proposes a compromise : he suggests that those who say Homer's poetry is pure ballad-poetry, and those who deny that it is ballad-poetry at all, should split the difference between them ; that it should be agreed that Homer's poems are ballads *a little*, but not so much as some have said. I am very sensible to the courtesy of the terms in which Mr. Blackie invites me to this compromise ; but I cannot, I am sorry to say, accept it ; I cannot allow that Homer's poetry is ballad-poetry at all. A want of capacity for sustained nobleness seems to me inherent in the ballad-form, when employed for epic poetry. The more we examine this proposition, the more certain, I think, will it become to us. Let us but observe how a great poet, having to deliver a

narrative very weighty and serious, instinctively
shrinks from the ballad-form as from a form not
commensurate with his subject-matter, a form too
narrow and shallow for it, and seeks for a form which
has more amplitude and impressiveness. Every one
knows the *Lucy Gray* and the *Ruth* of Wordsworth.
Both poems are excellent; but the subject-matter of
the narrative of *Ruth* is much more weighty and
impressive to the poet's own feeling than that of the
narrative of *Lucy Gray*, for which latter, in its un-
pretending simplicity, the ballad-form is quite adequate. Wordsworth, at the time he composed Ruth,—
his great time, his *annus mirabilis*, about 1800,—strove
to be simple; it was his mission to be simple; he
loved the ballad-form, he clung to it, because it was
simple. Even in *Ruth* he tried, one may say, to use
it; he would have used it if he could : but the gravity
of his matter is too much for this somewhat slight
form; he is obliged to give to his form more amplitude, more augustness, to shake out its folds.

> " The wretched parents all that night
>   Went shouting far and wide ;
> But there was neither sound nor sight
>   To serve them for a guide."

That is beautiful, no doubt, and the form is adequate
to the subject-matter. But take this, on the other
hand :—

> " I, too, have passed her on the hills,
>   Setting her little water-mills
>   By spouts and fountains wild ;
>   Such small machinery as she turned,
>   Ere she had wept, ere she had mourned,
>   A young and happy child."

Who does not perceive how the greater fulness and weight of his matter has here compelled the true and feeling poet to adopt a form of more *volume* than the simple ballad-form ?

It is of narrative poetry that I am speaking; the question is about the use of the ballad-form for *this*. I say that for this poetry (when in the grand style, as Homer's is) the ballad-form is entirely inadequate; and that Homer's translator must not adopt it, because it even leads him, by its own weakness, away from the grand style rather than towards it. We must remember that the matter of narrative poetry stands in a different relation to the vehicle which conveys it,—is not so independent of this vehicle, so absorbing and powerful in itself,—as the matter of purely emotional poetry. When there comes in poetry what I may call the *lyrical cry*, this trans-figures everything, makes everything grand; the simplest form may be here even an advantage, because the flame of the emotion glows through and through it more easily. To go again for an illustration to Wordsworth;—our great poet, since Milton, by his performance, as Keats, I think, is our great poet by his gift and promise;—in one of his stanzas to the Cuckoo, we have :—

> "And I can listen to thee yet ;
>   Can lie upon the plain
> And listen, till I do beget
>   That golden time again."

Here the lyrical cry, though taking the simple ballad-form, is as grand as the lyrical cry coming in poetry of an ampler form, as grand as the

> "An innocent life, yet far astray!"

of *Ruth ;* as the

> "There is a comfort in the strength of love"

of *Michael.* In this way, by the occurrence of this lyrical cry, the ballad-poets themselves rise sometimes, though not so often as one might perhaps have hoped, to the grand style.

> "O lang, lang may their ladies sit,
>   Wi' their fans into their hand,
>   Or ere they see Sir Patrick Spence
>   Come sailing to the land.
>
> "O lang, lang may the ladies stand,
>   Wi' their gold combs in their hair,
>   Waiting for their ain dear lords,
>   For they'll see them nae mair."

But from this impressiveness of the ballad-form, when its subject-matter fills it over and over again,—is, indeed, in itself, all in all,—one must not infer its effectiveness when its subject-matter is not thus over-powering, in the great body of a narrative.

But, after all, Homer is not a better poet than the balladists, because he has taken in the hexameter a better instrument ; he took this instrument because he was a *different* poet from them ; so different,—not only so much better, but so essentially different,—that he is not to be classed with them at all. Poets receive their distinctive character, not from their subject, but from their application to that subject of the ideas (to quote the *Excursion)*

> "On God, on Nature, and on human life,"

which they have acquired for themselves. In the

ballad-poets in general, as in men of a rude and early
stage of the world, in whom their humanity is not
yet variously and fully developed, the stock of these
ideas is scanty, and the ideas themselves not very
effective or profound.   From them the narrative
itself is the great matter, not the spirit and significance which underlies the narrative.   Even in later
times of richly developed life and thought, poets
appear who have what may be called a *balladist's
mind ;* in whom a fresh and lively curiosity for the
outward spectacle of the world is much more strong
than their sense of the inward significance of that
spectacle.   When they apply ideas to their narrative
of human events, you feel that they are, so to speak,
travelling out of their own province: in the best of
them you feel this perceptibly, but in those of a lower
order you feel it very strongly.   Even Sir Walter
Scott's efforts of this kind,—even, for instance, the

> " Breathes there the man with soul so dead,"

or the

> " O woman ! in our hours of ease,"—

even these leave, I think, as high poetry, much to be
desired ; far more than the same poet's descriptions
of a hunt or a battle.   But Lord Macaulay's

> " Then out spake brave Horatius,
>   The captain of the gate :
> ' To all the men upon this earth
>   Death cometh soon or late,' "

(and here, since I have been reproached with under-
valuing Lord Macaulay's *Lays of Ancient Rome*, let

me frankly say that, to my mind, a man's power to
detect the ring of false metal in those Lays is a good
measure of his fitness to give an opinion about
poetical matters at all),—I say, Lord Macaulay's

> "To all the men upon this earth
> Death cometh soon or late,"

it is hard to read without a cry of pain.   But with
Homer it is very different.   This "noble barbarian,"
this "savage with the lively eye,"—whose verse, Mr.
Newman thinks, would affect us, if we could hear the
living Homer, "like an elegant and simple melody
from an African of the Gold Coast,"—is never more
at home, never more nobly himself, than in applying
profound ideas to his narrative.   As a poet he belongs
—narrative as is his poetry, and early as is his date
—to an incomparably more developed spiritual and
intellectual order than the balladists, or than Scott
and Macaulay; he is here as much to be distinguished
from them, and in the same way, as Milton is to be
distinguished from them.   He is, indeed, rather to
be classed with Milton than with the balladists and
Scott; for what he has in common with Milton—the
noble and profound application of ideas to life—is the
most essential part of poetic greatness.   The most
essentially grand and characteristic things of Homer
are such things as—

> ἔτλην δ᾽, οἷ᾽ οὔπω τις ἐπιχθόνιος βροτὸς ἄλλος,
> ἀνδρὸς παιδοφόνοιο ποτὶ στόμα χεῖρ᾽ ὀρέγεσθαι,[1]

---

[1] "And I have endured—the like whereof no soul upon the
earth hath yet endured—to carry to my lips the hand of him
who slew my child."—*Iliad*, xxiv. 505.

or as—

κal σὲ, γέρον, τὸ πρὶν μὲν ἀκούομεν ὄλβιον εἶναι,[1]

or as—

ὡς γὰρ ἐπεκλώσαντο θεοὶ δειλοῖσι βροτοῖσιν,
ζώειν ἀχνυμένους · αὐτοὶ δέ τ' ἀκηδέες εἰσίν,[2]

and of these the tone is given, far better than by any
thing of the balladists, by such things as the

"Io no piangeva : sì dentro impietrai :
Piangevan elli . . ."[3]

of Dante ; or the

"Fall'n Cherub ! to be weak is miserable"

of Milton.

I suppose I must, before I conclude, say a word or
two about my own hexameters ; and yet really, on
such a topic, I am almost ashamed to trouble you.
From those perishable objects I feel, I can truly say,
a most Oriental detachment. You yourselves are
witnesses how little importance, when I offered them
to you, I claimed for them,—how humble a function
I designed them to fill. I offered them, not as specimens of a competing translation of Homer, but as
illustrations of certain canons which I had been trying to establish for Homer's poetry. I said that these

[1] "Nay and thou too, old man, in times past wert, as we
hear, happy."—*Iliad*, xxiv. 543. In the original this line, for
mingled pathos and dignity, is perhaps without a rival even in
Homer.

[2] "For so have the gods spun our destiny to us wretched
mortals,—that we should live in sorrow ; but they themselves
are without trouble."—*Iliad*, xxiv. 525.

[3] "*I* wept not : so of stone grew I within :—*they* wept."—
Hell, xxxiii. 49 (Carlyle's Translation, slightly altered).

canons they might very well illustrate by failing as
well as by succeeding : if they illustrate them in any
manner, I am satisfied.   I was thinking of the future
translator of Homer, and trying to let him see as
clearly as possible what I meant by the combination
of characteristics which I assigned to Homer's poetry,
—by saying that this poetry was at once rapid in
movement, plain in words and style, simple and direct
in its ideas, and noble in manner.   I do not suppose that my own hexameters are rapid in movement,
plain in words and style, simple and direct in their
ideas, and noble in manner; but I am in hopes that
a translator, reading them with a genuine interest in
his subject, and without the slightest grain of personal feeling, may see more clearly, as he reads them,
what I mean by saying that Homer's poetry is all
these.   I am in hopes that he may be able to seize
more distinctly, when he has before him my

"So shone forth, in front of Troy, by the bed of the Xanthus,"

or my

"Ah, unhappy pair, to Peleus why did we give you !"

or my

"So he spake, and drove with a cry his steeds into battle, "

the exact points which I wish him to avoid in Cowper's

"So numerous seemed those fires the banks between,"

or in Pope's

"Unhappy coursers of immortal strain,"

or in Mr. Newman's

"He spake, and, yelling, held a-front his single-hoofed horses."

At the same time there may be innumerable points in
mine which he ought to avoid also. Of the merit of
his own compositions no composer can be admitted
the judge.

But thus humbly useful to the future translator I
still hope my hexameters may prove; and he it is,
above all, whom one has to regard. The general
public carries away little from discussions of this
kind, except some vague notion that one advocates
English hexameters, or that one has attacked Mr.
Newman. On the mind of an adversary one never
makes the faintest impression. Mr. Newman reads
all one can say about diction, and his last word on
the subject is, that he "regards it as a question about
to open hereafter, whether a translator of Homer
ought not to adopt the old dissyllabic *landis, houndis,
hartis*" (for lands, hounds, harts), and also "the final
en of the plural of verbs (we *dancen*, they *singen*,
etc.)," which "still subsists in Lancashire." A certain
critic reads all one can say about style, and at the end
of it arrives at the inference that, "after all, there is
some style grander than the grand style itself, since
Shakspeare has not the grand manner, and yet has
the supremacy over Milton;" another critic reads all
one can say about rhythm, and the result is, that he
thinks Scott's rhythm, in the description of the death
of Marmion, all the better for being *saccadé*, because
the dying ejaculations of Marmion were likely to be
"jerky." How vain to rise up early, and to take rest
late, from any zeal for proving to Mr. Newman that
he must not, in translating Homer, say *houndis* and

dancen ; or to the first of the two critics above quoted, that one poet may be a greater poetical force than another, and yet have a more unequal style; or to the second, that the best art, having to represent the death of a hero, does not set about imitating his dying noises! Such critics, however, provide for an opponent's vivacity the charming excuse offered by Rivarol for his, when he was reproached with giving offence by it :—"Ah!" he exclaimed, "no one considers how much pain every man of taste has had to *suffer*, before he ever inflicts any."

It is for the future translator that one must work. The successful translator of Homer will have (or he cannot succeed) that true sense for his subject, and that disinterested love of it, which are, both of them, so rare in literature, and so precious; he will not be led off by any false scent; he will have an eye for the real matter, and, where he thinks he may find any indication of this, no hint will be too slight for him, no shade will be too fine, no imperfections will turn him aside,—he will go before his adviser's thought, and help it out with his own. This is the sort of student that a critic of Homer should always have in his thoughts; but students of this sort are indeed rare.

And how, then, can I help being reminded what a student of this sort we have just lost in Mr. Clough, whose name I have already mentioned in these lectures? He, too, was busy with Homer; but it is not on that account that I now speak of him. Nor do I speak of him in order to call attention to his qualities and powers in general, admirable as these were. I mention him because, in so eminent a degree, he possessed these two invaluable literary qualities,—a true sense for his object of study, and a single-hearted care for it.   He had both; but he had the second even more eminently than the first.   He greatly developed the first through means of the second.   In the study of art, poetry, or philosophy, he had the most undivided and disinterested love for his object in itself, the greatest aversion to mixing up with it anything accidental or personal.   His interest was in literature itself; and it was this which gave so rare a stamp to his character, which kept him so free from all taint of littleness.   In the saturnalia of ignoble personal passions, of which the struggle for literary success, in old and crowded communities, offers so sad a spectacle, he never mingled.   He had not yet traduced his friends, nor flattered his enemies, nor disparaged what he admired, nor praised what he despised. Those who knew him well had the conviction that, even with time, these literary arts would never be his.   His poem, of which I before spoke, has some admirable Homeric qualities;—out-of-doors freshness, life, naturalness, buoyant rapidity.   Some of the expressions in that poem,— "*Dangerous Corrievreckan . . . Where roads are unknown to Loch Nevish,*"—come back now to my ear with the true Homeric ring. But that in him of which I think oftenest is the Homeric simplicity of his literary life.

THE END OF VOL. II.